9.95

Test
Taking
Secrets

The Backpack Study Series

Backpack Study Secrets
Backpack Speed-Reading Secrets
Backpack Term Paper Secrets
Backpack Test-Taking Secrets

Test Taking Secrets

Study better, test smarter, and get great grades

Steven Frank

Adams Media Corporation
HOLBROOK, MASSACHUSETTS

Published by
Adams Media Corporation
260 Center Street, Holbrook, MA 02343

ISBN: 1-58062-027-2

Printed in Canada.

J I H G F E D C B A

Library of Congress Cataloging-in-Publication Data
Frank, Steven.
Test taking secrets/ Steven Frank.
p.   cm. — (Backpack study series)
ISBN 1-58062-027-2
1. Test-taking skills — United States. 2. Study skills — United States.
3. College students — Time management — United States. I. Title.
II. Series: Frank, Steven. Backpack study series.
LB30360.57.F73   1998
371.26— dc21   98-14120
CIP

This publication is designed to provide accurate and authoritative information with regard to the subject matter covered. It is sold with the understanding that the publisher is not engaged in rendering legal, accounting, or other professional advice. If legal advice or other expert assistance is required, the services of a competent professional person should be sought.
— From a *Declaration of Principles* jointly adopted by a Committee of the American Bar Association and a Committee of Publishers and Associations

This book is available at quantity discounts for bulk purchases.
For information, call 1-800-872-5627 (in Massachusetts, 781-767-8100).

Visit our home page at http://www.adamsmedia.com

Contents

Preface

When I was a sophomore in college, I pulled an all-nighter in order to study for a midterm examination in a class on Shakespeare. Until then, this had been my typical way of studying, and I had managed to pull decent grades. I spent the entire night reading over my notes and things I'd underlined in the textbook. With the help of about a dozen cups of coffee, I managed to stay up all night, although by 3 A.M. I was practically climbing the walls.

When I received the exam the next day in class, I was thrilled to see that the two essay questions were relatively easy. They both involved plays that I really knew well. I did an adequate job on the first essay, but something terrible happened on the second one. As I began my response, exhaustion hit me as hard as if I'd been knocked over by a hardcover edition of *The Complete Works of Shakespeare*. I knew what I wanted to write, but I just didn't have the energy to go through with writing the whole essay. I managed to scribble some basic ideas, but I was just too tired to take the time to back them up in detail. Even though there was a half-hour left of the examination — plenty of time in which to finish the essay — I turned in my exam booklet and went home to get some sleep.

Later, after I'd napped and was at last thinking like a rational and sane human being, I got angry at myself. I knew the answer to that question and could have written a dyna-mite essay. But because of the way I'd spent the night study-ing, I had inadvertently sabotaged myself. I would have been better off, I realized, not having studied at all than staying up all night. There just had to be a better way to study.

Over the course of the rest of my education, as both an undergraduate and graduate student, I experimented with various techniques and strategies for studying more effec-tively and efficiently. The strategies included in this book are the ones I found to be most successful. Many of these tech-niques I learned the hard way, through plain old trial and error. Others, though, I learned by talking to people who were themselves highly successful students. Based on the many things I've seen and heard from these students and experienced myself, I've compiled these basic strategies.

Through my experiences teaching college students, I have gained insight into the teacher's point of view of the educational process. I now have a much more accurate sense, for example, of the kinds of things that impress teachers most in their students on exams. I have incorpo-rated these insights into the discussion of study and test-taking skills throughout the book.

Introduction

Are You One of These Students?

The Mad Crammer

Although the Mad Crammer tries to make it to most of his classes, he doesn't bother doing any work outside of class, like reading his notes or the required assignments. He figures there'll be plenty of time for all that later in the semester. Before he knows it, finals week has arrived and he's got only two days to prepare for four exams. Drinking coffee by the gallon, he stays awake night and day poring over his books, trying to force himself to remember as much as he can. He shows up at his first exam bleary eyed, with a killer headache. When the exam is passed out, he can barely read the questions let alone answer them. Much of the material on the exam looks vaguely familiar, but when he tries to remember more exact information, everything becomes muddled together in his mind. When he gets to the essay section, he's relieved to see the question relates to material he had read just the night before. He begins writing, but after a few paragraphs, he is completely exhausted and just doesn't have the energy to continue.

The Midexam Panicker

Unlike the Mad Crammer, the Midexam Panicker methodically prepares for an upcoming exam. She begins studying two weeks before finals and goes into the first exam confident she'll ace it. She breezes through the first section, all multiple choice questions. But when she comes to the first essay, she is horrified to find that she doesn't understand the question at all. She starts to feel sick to her stomach as her pulse begins to race. Figuring she'll come back to the question later on, she goes on to the next essay question. She begins to write, but all she can think about is that other question she skipped. How many points was it worth? Will she fail the exam? Will she fail the course? Will she have to drop out of school? Will she ever get a job if they hear about how she did on this exam? Unable to write, she keeps thinking and thinking about that one question, right up until the proctor announces that time is up.

The Alarmist

Whenever the Alarmist sees someone from his class, he corners them and launches into his typical speech: "I heard that Professor Abrams's exams are just impossible. Last year like thirty people failed the exam. I don't see how I'm going to pass. How are you going to pass? What have you studied? Have you studied Chapter 12? I heard Chapter 12 is the one Abrams always asks questions on. Oh, and you better study all the charts in the appendix, because I heard he asked about that last year. And I heard that this year's exam is going to be the hardest ever." When the exams are returned, the Alarmist is surprised to find he did quite well. Three of the people he had spoken to before the exam, though, failed. They had spent the entire night studying Chapter 12, which was never on the exam.

Going the Distance

Many students think that acing an exam is merely a question of how naturally intelligent they are, or how much they can cram, memorize, and spit back out once in the exam. However, as the preceding examples indicate, there's a lot more to succeeding on tests than reading and memorization. If you don't prepare for an examination the right way and go in with a confident attitude, you can be in for some trouble.

An exam is just as much a test of mental and physical endurance as it is your knowledge of a particular subject. In that sense, it's somewhat akin to running a marathon. Even though most marathon runners run some distance every day, during the weeks before a major race they move their training into high gear, running longer hours and further distances so they will be ready for the upcoming event.

Before a test, you too should move your studying into high gear, focusing your energy more on the subject matter. The methods and strategies outlined here will help you do that. The more advanced training and preparation a marathon runner has, the smoother a race he or she will run, and the greater a chance of success. This book is designed to provide you with the extensive training and preparation for an exam that will make your "test run" on exam day also a smooth and successful one. If you follow the strategies described in this book, you'll be so well-prepared for an exam, you won't have to sweat about it. You'll be able to answer virtually any exam question, even be able to write your own entire exam. But we will also discuss special tips and strategies you can call upon during an exam to improve your performance.

Active Studying

The key to effective test preparation is making the study process more *active*. Although they don't realize it, many students approach studying in a passive manner. They think that as long as they look at their notes and read their textbooks they are covering the material adequately. Studying, in this sense, is not much different from watching television: You simply look, listen, and somehow "take it all in." But you probably are never going to have an exam on a particular television show.

The material you study in school, though, is different; you *will* be tested on it, and you'll need to recall information in great detail. Sitting back and "taking it all in" is therefore not going to cut it.

Rather than approaching studying in this passive manner, this book shows that the secret to study success is studying actively. *Active* studying means you *do* something. Instead of merely looking at your notes and trying to remember as much of the course material as you can, you *think, write, ask questions, answer questions, and brainstorm in creative ways.* In the process, you become comfortable with the material you've learned, so comfortable that it is a part of your general knowledge. As a result, you are better able to retain the information for exams and use it to answer questions of all kinds.

You'll find that all the strategies in the book include methods to involve you actively in your studies. In a general sense, though, you need to establish yourself as an active student right from the start. That means acknowledging that your education, especially around exam time, involves work — hard work. Even though you might be sitting at a desk or lying on the couch reading over notes, your mind must remain hard at work. As soon as you slip into a passive mode, the material before you will be lost and you might as well have been watching television.

You don't need to be a bookworm or genius to get good grades on tests, but you do need to be a "chariot of fire," willing to train hard with the goal of getting to that exam and acing it. Don't be like the students outlined. As exams approach, make the commitment to go into active test training. After you do, you'll be more than ready for whatever bumps and hurdles await you during the actual test run.

Advance Preparations

Follow a Regimen: Train All Year

Although you'll go into more intensive training in the days just before an exam, you should think of yourself as being in training for exams *throughout the entire school term.* In many ways, you can put yourself on the path to exam success starting on the first day of class. Exams, after all, are partly designed to test just how much you've learned and retained from a particular course. That means it's extremely important that you expose yourself to as much of the course material — class lectures and discussions, reading assignments — as possible. In fact, if you can manage to attend every class and keep up with every reading assignment, you'll already have begun the process of preparing for an exam and probably helped improve your performance.

On the other hand, the more classes you miss and reading assignments you skip, the more you'll have to try to accomplish right before an exam. That creates unnecessary

Be an active student in training for upcoming exams all term. Keep up with reading assignments and attend as many classes as you can.

stress that can lead to panic and diminish your performance. Moreover, by cramming the material at the very last moment, you lose the benefit of having repeated exposure. When you keep up regularly with the course work, you become engaged with the material on a regular, repeated basis. This can help you become much more in tune with and knowledgeable of the entire subject, as well as various topics covered within it. That familiarity breeds confidence, making studying for and taking the exam much less stressful.

Try to attend every class and to keep up with every reading assignment. If you are forced to miss a class, make certain you do your best to find out what was covered in as much detail as possible. You should arrange to borrow and copy a friend's notes — or even notes from a few different people, as they may have each taken notes on different parts of the class. You should not only copy the notes but also make sure you read them over carefully and that you fully understand them. If you don't, talk to people from the class, or even arrange to meet with the professor to make certain you do in fact understand everything that was discussed. If you know in advance you must miss a class, you can arrange to have a friend tape record it. That way you can hear for yourself everything that was covered.

If you've got heaps of work to do and have to skip some reading assignments, try to find the time later in the semester when you can catch up. Do this, if you can, well before the exam. That way, you still have time to read the assignment over carefully and begin to process the information into your memory.

In addition to attending classes and keeping up with reading assignments, it is also important that you take notes as you go. These notes provide important materials to help you in your preparation for an exam. Rather than having to reread all those lengthy reading assignments or struggle to remember exactly what a teacher covered in a lecture, you'll have a concise and accessible set of notes from which to study.

The other books in the Backpack Study Series offer a variety of tips and strategies for study tasks, including taking notes in class and on reading assignments. If you follow these strategies, you'll be able to create detailed, accurate sets of notes from your classroom lectures and reading assignments that will be instrumental in preparing for an exam. Moreover, the actual process of taking the notes throughout the term is itself a study technique that helps prepare you for an exam. Taking notes using these strategies encourages you to be a more active student — working with and thinking about concepts relevant to the course all semester. You thus gain a comfortable familiarity with the subject, making it an integrated part of your overall knowledge, and are ready to apply that knowledge to whatever questions are posed to you.

> If you miss class, make certain you find out what was covered. If you skip a reading, try to make it up at some point when you have more time.

Know What You're In For

One of the things that causes panic or stress in any situation is fear of the unknown. If you don't know what's lurking behind a door, you might very well be afraid to open it, especially when your imagination goes to work and transforms whatever is behind that door into a ax-wielding maniac. Your imagination can also convince you that an upcoming exam will include killer questions impossible to get right. You can put your mind at ease, though, by finding out as much as you can about an upcoming exam *before* you go into the examination room.

In addition to alleviating panic, knowing something about the format of an exam can help you plan your study schedule more efficiently. As you'll soon see, there are different ways to study for different types of examination questions. If you have an idea of the kinds of questions likely to be on an examination, you can tailor your study schedule specifically to preparing for those questions.

Types of Exam Questions

Exam questions generally fall into two categories: short answer and "longer" answer questions, such as essays and problem sets.

4

Short answer questions are designed to test your knowledge — quickly and broadly — of a specific subject. Most questions of this type are straightforward tests of your factual knowledge; essentially, you either know the answer or you do not. However, some can be more complex, requiring that you apply concepts to other areas, or respond with the answer that is *most* correct. When exams include short answer sections, there will generally be a large number of questions, each worth only a few points. That can be encouraging, as you then know that if you cannot answer some questions, you will not blow the entire exam.

The basic types of short answer questions are:

True/False. These are the easiest type of short answer question. You are given a statement and must determine if it is correct or incorrect. You thus have a fifty percent chance of getting the right answer.

> *EXAMPLE*
> *True or False?*
>
> ___ *A simile is when an animal or object is described as possessing human characteristics.*
>
> ___ *"O my love's like a red, red rose" is an example of a simile.*

Multiple Choice. Multiple choice questions are those for which you are given a question or statement followed by a series of possible answers; out of those possibilities, you must provide the correct response. These are more difficult than true/false questions in that there are several possible answers to choose from, only one of which is right.

Many multiple choice questions are based on identifying some kind of relationship between different ideas and terms. For example, many multiple choice questions ask you to identify an example of some principle, theory or idea.

> *EXAMPLE*
> *Which of the following is an example of a simile?*
>
> *a. "O my love's like a red, red rose"*
> *b. "Death, be not proud, though some have called thee"*
> *c. "Beauty is truth, truth beauty"*
> *d. "Shall I compare thee to a summer's day?"*

Sometimes, you might have to do the opposite, and identify the larger principle a particular example illustrates.

> *EXAMPLE*
> *"O my love's like a red, red rose" is an example of which type of figurative language?*
>
> *a. personification*
> *b. metaphor*
> *c. simile*
> *d. hyperbole*

These questions can become more complicated when you need to identify several examples of a particular principle or theory and/or eliminate others that don't apply.

> *EXAMPLE*
>   I. *"O my love's like a red, red rose"*
> II. *"Higher still and higher/From the earth thou springest/Like a cloud of fire"*
> III. *"Beauty is truth, truth beauty"*
> IV. *"Shall I compare thee to a summer's day?"*
>
> *Which of the above is/are example(s) of a simile?*
>
>   *a. I and II only*
>   *b. III and IV only*
>   *c. all of the above*
>   *d. none of the above*

Matching. For this section of an exam, you are given two lists of terms or phrases; you are expected to connect each item in the first column with one in the second column to which it is most logically connected. For example, in a foreign language class, you might be given a list of terms in the foreign language and are expected to match each with its English translation from the second column. These questions are tricky in that if you mismatch one or more terms, you can have difficulty with the entire section. At the same time, though, for each term you correctly match, you successfully narrow down the list of remaining possibilities.

Take careful and accurate notes in classes and on reading assignments (if you like, following the strategies outlined in the *Study Secrets* and *Reading Secrets*). These help you begin to learn and retain information throughout the term; they also provide you with the materials you'll need from which to study for exams.

EXAMPLE
Match the literary term on the left with an example of it from the column on the right.

____ *a. personification*   1. *O my love's like a red, red rose*

____ *b. simile*   2. *his brilliance was far greater*
                                        than that of the sun

____ *c. metaphor*   3. *the clouds were in a dark mood*

____ *d. hyperbole*   4. *his fiery anger scorched his*
                                        own heart

Fill in the Blank. For these questions, you are given a statement or paragraph in which a word, term, or phrase is missing; you are expected to write the correct information in the blank. Unlike multiple choice questions, you are not given a list of possible answers, making these short answer questions the most difficult. For these, you truly must know the correct answer on your own.

EXAMPLE
"O my love's like a red, red rose" is an example of a

_____.

8

Essays/Problem Sets. Unlike short answer questions, essays and problem solving sections are generally worth more points and require you to do much more work on the actual exam. You cannot quickly and easily check off or fill in an answer.

Essays require that you write an extended, organized response to some question. You are expected to provide detailed, correct information in support of your particular analysis or response, in a manner that is clear yet sophisticated, demonstrating your mastery of the subject matter.

EXAMPLES

Write a detailed essay in which you identify and compare the factors and events that led to the French Revolution with those that resulted in the American Revolution for Independence. What were the philosophical arguments used to justify the wars? What were the specific economic and historical developments that directly sparked these wars?

What are the primary characteristics that distinguish the romantic poets? In your response, discuss specifically three poems by three different romantic poets.

For some classes, especially in science and mathematics, you might have to work on a set of problems, employing formulas, theorems, and scientific/mathematic principles to come up with correct answers. Sometimes, you will work on problems within a short answer framework; you'll have to figure out the problem,

> Some teachers are quite creative when it comes to writing questions and creating exam formats. That's why it is worth the effort to try and find out what awaits you.

but you will also have to choose from a set of possible answers. At other times, especially for testing more complex principles, you might have to work out a complicated problem and demonstrate the steps you followed in solving the problem. In certain respects, this is the equivalent of writing an essay; rather than providing an extensive prose response, you are showing the extensive work you put into finding the answer.

EXAMPLE
Examine the following lists and charts detailing grade points for thirty students on a series of examinations. Based on those statistics, compute the mean, variance, standard deviation, and margin of error.

Getting Advance Information

Here are some ways to find out about an upcoming exam:

Talk to the Professor. The most obvious source for information about an exam is the professor; after all, the professor is the one who makes up the questions. Most professors will take a few minutes during a class to explain the format and the material to be covered on an upcoming exam. Your course syllabus might also describe the exam. If an exam is approaching and the professor has not made such an announcement or described the exam, you can take the initiative. Raise your hand, and ask.

Although you can ask about an upcoming exam in class, talking to the professor after class or during office hours is, in some ways, more effective. Outside of class, the professor will probably be more inclined to talk with you at length since it's not taking up other students' time. You'll therefore be able to ask more questions and, if you're lucky, the professor might offer you more detailed information about the exam than he would in class.

These are some basic questions you can ask a professor about an upcoming exam:

- What will be the format? Will there be short answer questions? What type? Multiple choice questions? Will there be essays? A combination of types of questions?
- How many sections will there be? How many points will each section be worth?
- How much of your overall grade does the exam count for?
- What material from class will be covered?
- If the exam is a final, will it be cumulative (meaning it covers the entire semester's worth of material)? Or will it only cover a portion of the course material?
- Does the professor have any suggestions as to the best way to study for the exam?

Try to see the professor at least one week before a scheduled exam; that gives you enough time to plan your study schedule accordingly. However, there's no reason why you can't ask about an exam much earlier in the semester. While the professor may not have made up the exam yet, she probably has an idea of what the overall format will be and the material it covers. If you get this information early on, you can keep it in mind throughout the course and always be on the lookout for possible exam questions as you take notes from classroom lectures and readings.

Study Previous Exams. In addition to talking to the professor, you can get a highly accurate sense of what an upcoming exam will be like by looking at previous exams. In addition to providing examples of the kinds of questions likely to be included, you can use old examinations as practice runs to test yourself on the course material.

Some departments keep exams on file so that students may use them as a study resource. You can also try to find a friend or acquaintance who already took the course and held onto the exams and is willing to lend them to you. Just make certain that you are not doing anything unethical in looking at old examinations. If the professor has given a graded exam back to the students, then she knows it is available for anyone to examine. However, if the professor collects the exams and does not return them, then she doesn't intend for them to be distributed among students. If you somehow get a pirated copy of an exam, you are committing a serious breach of ethics that can get you in big trouble. When you consider the penalties, you'll realize that it's just not worth the risk; there are plenty of other study resources you can use without having to worry.

Ideally you want to find an old exam for the same course you are taking that was made up by your professor. This provides you with the most accurate picture of the exam you can expect to take. If you can't find an old exam written by your professor, you can try to track down exams for the same course given by other professors. Although these exams might not include the exact questions your own teacher has asked, they will provide you with a general sense of the types of questions frequently asked on exams in that subject. It also makes it easier to find old exams when you don't limit your search to your own professor. For example, you can borrow exams from friends at other schools who have taken the same course.

You can also learn a great deal by looking at exams your own professor has given in the past for *other* courses. While you may not get any clues as to the exact questions likely to appear on your upcoming exam, you will get a sense of the kinds of questions your professor asks and the overall level of difficulty of her exams.

Once you have one exam for a course, it can give you an indication of what to expect from upcoming exams. Professors and teachers tend to have a consistent examination style, preferring certain formats and questions. Upcoming exams will likely resemble earlier ones in terms of the type of questions and overall level of difficulty. When you get an exam back, look it over carefully to figure out what kind of exam writer your teacher is. You can also try

Get as much information about an upcoming test from the teacher; watch carefully for "clues" during class discussions and lectures.

to identify those types of questions on which you tend to succeed, and those that present problems.

Listen for Clues. Throughout the semester, keep your ears open for any clues as to what might be included on an exam. Clues can crop up any time, so be on the lookout. A professor might say, in a completely casual manner, that a particular concept or term is likely to show up on the exam. After making a certain point, a teacher might say something like, "If I were to ask a question on an exam about this topic, I'd ask you...." Any time your professor makes any reference to an exam, even in an off-hand manner, make certain you make a note of it and star it.

In addition to blatant references to exams, the professor will probably give you other subtle clues. Exam questions always reflect the professor's personal interests and biases. Even if the course is a basic survey course, there are certain to be some topics your teacher feels are more important for you to know and are therefore more likely to show up on an exam. Anything your professor seems particularly serious or passionate about is a likely candidate for inclusion on an exam. Any point your professor has made repeatedly, or given special attention to, is also more likely to appear on an exam. Star these points in your notes to remind yourself to study them before an exam.

Test Training Step 1:
Reread and Reorganize
Your Notes

*I*n this and the next several chapters, you'll learn about an effective strategy for preparing for an exam. Following this strategy ensures you prepare for an exam in an active fashion; you'll truly retain the information you study and be able to apply that information to exam questions. The basic steps in this strategy are:

> **Step 1: Reread and Reorganize Your Notes**
> — **Reread All Notes from Lectures and Readings**
> — **Create Three Master-Lists from Notes**
>   **Master-List of Key Terms**
>   **Master-List of General Themes and Topics**
>   **Master-List of Related Concepts**

Step 2: Work with the Master-Lists
— Master-Lists and Exam Questions
— Quiz Yourself
— Brainstorm Your Own Exam Questions

Step 3: Get Help When You Need It

Reread All Notes from Lectures and Readings

Many students begin to panic before an exam because they've left themselves way too much to worry about at the last minute. An examination approaches, and they find they still have to read assignments they never got to, reread assignments they don't remember, scrounge up notes for lectures they missed, and figure out what their own notes mean if they've forgotten.

The first step in this test training strategy is rereading and reorganizing all of your notes from classroom lectures and reading assignments. To do this, you must have taken notes throughout the semester. You can follow strategies from the other Backpack Study Series books for taking these notes, which particularly lend themselves to the test preparation strategies described in this book. However, even if you do not use these specific strategies, make certain you have kept up with work throughout the term and taken some kind of notes. It's also important that you have these notes neatly organized in one location; that way, you know exactly where they are now that you need them. You

Make test preparation an active process. Do something active in addition to reading and reviewing notes.

won't have to start digging through your piles of books and papers to find notes and study materials.

To begin studying for an upcoming exam, gather together all of your notes from the course in one binder. This will not be a problem if you make it a point to put all of your notes in a binder at home throughout the semester. Just make certain you now have them all in one place, in a logical order.

The first step in the examination process is to read your notes from start to finish. It is extremely important that you do this in one sitting *without interruption*. This will help you concentrate more intently on the material; more importantly, it will enable you to develop a clear picture in your mind of the course material as a whole. Rather than studying various bits and pieces of information related to the subject, you'll now be able to see how everything fits together as part of the overall course.

For each examination, set aside several hours to read through your notes from beginning to end. However, don't study several subjects at once or one subject right after another. If you study several courses within a short period of time, the material can easily become mixed up and muddled in your mind, making it more difficult for you to remember specific details. Make certain you take a break of at least two hours before sitting down to read notes from another course.

Create Three Master-Lists from Notes

As you read over your notes from classroom lectures and reading assignments, you are now going to condense and reorganize the material onto three single sheets of paper — the three Master-Lists. The preparation of these lists is itself a major and effective part of the study process. First, the Master-Lists serve as your primary study tools; rather than having to read through all of your notes again and again, you only need to examine these three sheets. As we'll see in later sections, each Master-List prepares you for a specific kind of examination question.

Additionally, reorganizing your notes and other material from the course in this manner is an active study technique. Rather than just rereading, you are working while you read, thereby gaining a firmer grasp on the subject. You are also moving closer to an exam format. Most exams, after all, present the same information you first encountered in your class lectures and reading assignments in a new format. The more you become accustomed to reworking and rethinking material from a course, the more prepared you are to recognize and understand it in the context of an exam question.

The Master-List of Key Terms

Much of the new information you encounter while taking a course — either in classroom lectures and discussions or reading assignments — centers on *key terms*. Key terms are any words, names, or brief phrases that are important to and clearly related to a particular subject matter. Key terms

> Take detailed notes throughout the term. Have them in order and accessible for when you need to study for an exam.

might be names of people and places, important dates, texts and documents, theories, or formulas. Very often, these terms will be new to you. Even if you are already familiar with a term, you might learn much more during a semester about the term's significance in relation to the particular subject you are studying.

Any terms that a professor writes on the board, or repeats several times, or provides an extensive explanation of, are likely to be key terms worth noting and remembering. In reading assignments, especially in textbooks, key terms are often in boldface or italics. In general, any terms or phrases that are new to you and seem significant, are also worth noting. Many examination questions, as you'll see, also center on key terms.

One stage of reorganizing your notes is to create a Master-List of all of these key terms from which you can then study for exams. As you read through all your notes, write down the key terms — that means any names, dates, words, phrases, formulas, concepts, or ideas that are new to you and/or central to the course — without any definition or explanation of them. Try to squeeze all the key terms on a single sheet of paper. Don't write down any of the terms more than once; if a key term comes up repeatedly throughout the course, you only need to write it down once on your Master-List. You may also decide to eliminate some terms from the Master-List because you'll realize as you study that they aren't all that important.

If you've been following the note-taking methods outlined in *Study Secrets* and *Reading Secrets*, then you have already looked for and listed key terms in your notes from classroom lectures and reading assignments. You should still create this Master-List as it will be somewhat different from your notes. Unlike in your notes, you want this list to include only the terms without any definitions or explanations. You also want to edit the list down to fit on one piece of paper; that means determining which terms are the most important.

If you have not followed these strategies for listing key terms all semester, then you will have to work a bit more to identify key terms to create the Master-List. In addition to looking for the terms in any notes you've taken, you might want to brainstorm a bit; sit with a piece of paper, think back on everything you've studied and discussed for the course, and write down any names or terms that come to mind. You might also flip through reading assignments or handouts and write down any terms you spot, especially those in italics or bold, as these are usually particularly relevant and important.

The Master-List of General Themes and Topics

As you prepare for an exam and read through all of your notes, you should also create a Master-List of General Themes and Topics.

Generally, each class lecture and each reading assignment within a particular course will focus on some major

> Start by rereading all of your notes from beginning to end.

topic or theme; you can usually identify this topic or theme pretty easily. It might be listed on the course syllabus, or be the title of a textbook chapter. Within the lecture or reading assignment, several additional topics will be addressed, or certain themes — meaning main ideas or principles — will recur. These might be noted by the teacher on the blackboard or appear as subheadings within a textbook chapter. If not, you can still listen for and list whatever topics and themes crop up. You'll see in the next chapter how these themes often generate exam questions, especially for essays.

To prepare the Master-List of General Themes and Topics, you compile all of these themes/topics from the entire course on a single piece of paper. If a particular theme recurs throughout the course, you don't need to write it down more than once on the Master-List. However, you should put a star beside any recurring theme to indicate it is particularly important.

Throughout the course, just as you've been taking notes and writing down key terms, you should also have been noting the general themes and topics covered in each lecture and reading assignment. If you follow the Backpack Study Series strategies, you will have already done this, making it easy to now compile the Master-List. If not, you might have to brainstorm a bit. Flip through any notes you did take, look over the course syllabus, and glance through reading assignments and handouts. Then sit with a blank sheet of paper, think about everything you studied, and list whatever topics or themes occur to you.

The Master-List of Related Concepts

Creating this particular Master-List is a bit more complicated and will likely take more thought and effort than the other two. However, it will prove especially helpful in preparing for examination questions of all kinds.

As you read through your notes, try to identify groups of concepts and/or key terms that relate closely to one another. If you've identified such a group, write it down on the Master-List of Related Concepts and give it a subject heading. Beneath the subject heading, list all of the topics, themes, and terms that relate to that larger subject category.

A common category of related concepts is a principle or idea and the various examples that illustrate or support it. For example, you might be taking a history course in which the professor has argued repeatedly that the latter half of the Middle Ages was marked by an increased pessimism and despair. You might then group together the various events your professor described that indicate this trend:

Reasons for Increased Pessimism in the 14th and 15th Century

- *Weak kings (Edward II, Richard II) whose power was threatened by the barons*
- *Hundred Years War*

- *The Black Plague (1348)*
- *Skepticism in the Church (after sale of pardons is sanctioned)*

Here are other ways to group related concepts together that you might include on your Master-List:

- Events and Their Causes
- Rules and Exceptions
- Similar Ideas, Concepts, Theories, and Examples
- Opposite or Dissimilar Ideas, Concepts, Theories, and Examples
- Chronologies/Datelines
- Causes and Effects

Try to identify and write down as many of these groups of related concepts as you can. However, don't feel you have to identify every single one. There are actually a variety of ways to organize ideas and you won't likely be able to pick up on each one. However, the process of reorganizing your notes this way encourages you to think using the same kind of logic behind many examination questions. Creating this list involves rethinking what you learned in a logical manner; you also begin to apply certain concepts to other topics and subjects. As we'll see, creating this list helps you prepare for exam questions of all kinds, from short answer questions to essays.

You might have trouble, at first, fitting all of the groups of related concepts you identify on a single sheet of paper.

As you read, reorganize your notes by making three Master-Lists:

- Key Terms — list any significant terms, names, or phrases on which the course material focuses.
- General Themes and Topics — list any major points covered throughout a course in classes and lectures, especially those that are repeated.
- Related Concepts — tie together various themes, topics, and key points into categories for which you provide subject headings.

If this is the case, use more than one sheet. As you work more with the Master-List, you can make decisions about what to eliminate and eventually condense the list onto a single sheet.

Test Training Step 2:
Work with the Master-Lists

Step 1: Reread and Reorganize Your Notes
   — Reread All Notes from Lectures and Readings
   — Create Three Master-Lists from Notes

Step 2: Work with the Master-Lists
   — **Master-Lists and Exam Questions**
   — **Quiz Yourself**
   — **Brainstorm Your Own Exam Questions**

Step 3: Get Help When You Need It

After rereading and reorganizing of all your notes following the strategies outlined in the preceding chapter, you should now have created three separate Master-Lists: Key Terms, General Themes and Topics, and Related Concepts. The bulk of your preparation for the exam now centers on working with these Master-Lists.

First, let's look at exactly how each Master-List includes information that will help you answer a particular type of exam question. Then, we'll talk about ways to work with the Master-Lists so that you can retain information from them that you can use on the actual exam.

Master-Lists and Types of Exam Questions

Questions: Key Terms

Many short answer questions, such as true/false, multiple choice, matching, and fill-in-the-blank questions, are specifically designed to test you on your factual knowledge, to see if you know the meaning of or something of significance about a particular term. You can't figure out the answer to these questions using reasoning or other kinds of intellectual skills. Either you know the answer or you don't.

All of the following sample questions test factual knowledge based on key terms:

An elegy is:

1. *a poetic inscription that ends with a witty turn of thought.*
2. *a fourteen-line poem written in iambic pentameter.*
3. *a formal poetic lament after the death of a particular person.*
4. *a long narrative poem documenting heroic actions.*

A fourteen-line poem written in iambic pentameter is:

1. a sonnet.
2. an epigram.
3. an epic.
4. an elegy.

A _____ is a long narrative poem documenting heroic actions.

While short answer questions might specifically test you on factual knowledge, you'll also often need to know these facts to write essays. As we'll soon see, your primary goal in answering an essay question is to demonstrate to the professor your knowledge and mastery of the subject matter. Therefore, the more key terms you weave into an essay answer, the more you will impress the teacher with your knowledge.

For this reason, becoming very familiar with the key terms from the course is a crucial part of preparing for an examination. For some key terms, you need to be able to define them, to know exactly what they mean. For others, the term itself is nothing new, but you need to know something relevant *about* it in terms of its significance in the course. This is particularly the case with names of people, places, characters, and dates. For example, on a psychology exam, you might need to define the term "id." However, you might also need to know significant facts about Freud, such as the fact that he conceived of the model of human personality consisting of the id, ego, and superego.

Therefore, as part of your exam preparation, you should spend a certain amount of time learning and testing yourself on the key terms using the strategies outlined later in this chapter.

Questions: General Themes and Topics

While the Master-List of Key Terms includes many of the new and important terms you learned in a particular course, the Master-List of General Themes and Topics documents the main ideas and specific points covered for the course, such as points and perspectives that were addressed repeatedly in class and your readings. While preparing for an examination, the list of General Themes and Topics can give you insight into what you should study in detail; test questions almost always relate to the general themes rather than to the more obscure points. You can therefore examine the Master-List to determine the main subject areas for the course and focus your studying primarily on those key terms and concepts that relate to the General Themes.

The Master-List of General Themes can also be a valuable tool in preparing for essay examinations. Short answer questions are fairly limited in scope; each short answer question focuses on some specific piece of information. An essay question, though, requires that you elaborate at length on some topic related to the course. While answers to short answer questions are often key terms or phrases, responses to essay questions must be several paragraphs long. And unlike some short answer questions that provide you with possible answers to choose from, the entire essay comes from a single source — you.

An essay question must therefore be relatively broad so that a typical student in the class will be able to write a great deal about it. It will usually not be on some obscure point because your professor recognizes that you don't have the capacity to discuss it in any kind of detail. Instead, it will almost always refer to a major aspect of the course that you now have the ability to examine and discuss at length. In other words, an essay question almost always reflects one or more general themes or topics from the course.

Sometimes, an essay question may merely be a simple reworking of a general theme or topic from the course. For example, if you are taking a course on Shakespeare, a general theme might be: "Shakespeare's Experimentations with Genre" and specific topics might be, "Tragedy vs. Comedy" and "Plays that Defy or Challenge Easy Categorization." Possible essay questions that might then emerge from that question are:

- Discuss how Shakespeare experimented with the concept of genre.
- Choose three Shakespearean plays and discuss how they demonstrate Shakespeare experimenting with traditional forms of genre.
- *Romeo and Juliet* is commonly considered an example of Shakespearean tragedy. However, there are a number of elements in it more common in the comedies. Write an essay in which you discuss the comic aspects of *Romeo and Juliet*.

The first sample question essentially restates the general theme from the course into an essay topic. Although the other questions are much more specific in terms of what they ask you to discuss, they still relate to the general theme and other topics involving the genre of Shakespeare's plays.

As you'll see below, in addition to using this Master-List to focus your studying, you can also use it to brainstorm possible essay questions. By considering possible essays in advance, you are then better prepared to write an essay in class; you won't have to waste valuable time figuring out what to write, and which topics, terms, and examples are relevant to that particular question.

Questions: Related Concepts

As we have shown, many short answer questions test factual knowledge; either you know the answer or you don't. However, many are more complex, testing your ability to apply concepts to specific questions, or identify some kind of relationship between different ideas and terms.

For example, a multiple choice question might ask you to identify an example of some principle, theory, or idea:

Which of the following is an example of a defense mechanism?

1. *subliminal perception*
2. *schizophrenia*
3. *reaction formation*
4. *interposition*

You might have encountered the various terms in the above question during separate lectures and reading assignments. You now, perhaps for the first time, have to apply the larger idea of a defense mechanism to specific terms you might have studied in a very different context.

Sometimes, you might have to do the opposite, and identify the larger principle a particular example illustrates:

"I don't hate my brother. I really, really love my brother. I want to be with him all the time." This type of thinking is an example of which type of psychological phenomenon?

1. *schizophrenia*
2. *defense mechanism*
3. *interposition*
4. *subliminal perception*

These questions can become more complicated when you need to identify several examples of a particular principle or theory and/or eliminate others that don't apply:

I. *projection*
II. *denial*
III. *displacement*
IV. *reaction formation*

Which of the above is/are example(s) of defense mechanisms?

a. *I and II only*
b. *III and IV only*
c. *all of the above*
d. *none of the above*

Study the Master-Lists in an active fashion. Quiz yourself repeatedly on them, until you can say something significant about each term, topic, and concept on the lists.

For all these questions, you need to do more than be able to define the key terms; you need a sense of which terms go together and why. That's where the Master-List of Related Concepts comes in. By creating this list, you've begun thinking with the same logic and in the same terms as the exam questions.

The Master-List of Related Concepts is also helpful in preparing for essay questions. In the course of writing an essay, you may need to discuss a particular concept in detail. The Master-List helps you to identify the various topics, terms, ideas, and examples that support a particular concept, providing you with detailed information you can include in an essay response.

You can also use this Master-List to prepare for exams on which you'll have to work on math and science problems. Most problem solving depends on your knowledge of some theorem, formula, law, or principle. You can compile a Master-List for your course listing all of the math or science theorems, formulas, laws, and/or principles you've studied. Beneath each one, you can then list all of the types of problems to which those ideas might apply. When you see those types of problems on the exam, you should then instantly be able to recognize the theorem or formula you need to use to solve the problem.

Quiz Yourself

After you complete the Master-Lists, you need to take the time to go over them very carefully. In addition to reading them, you need to work with them actively so that you can absorb and retain information from them.

In general, you should continually quiz yourself on the Master-Lists. Try talking your way through each one, saying as much as you can about each term, topic, and concept. You can also try taking blank sheets of paper and attempting to replicate the three Master-Lists. The more you can remember, the more information you have absorbed.

Any time you come across a term or topic about which you are uncertain or that you cannot remember in detail, make a note of it. You can then go back to your original notes or reading assignments and find more detailed information about it. If that does not help, you can seek out additional information and extra help from sources outlined in the next chapter.

The following sections offer some specific ways to work with each Master-List.

Working with the Master-List of Key Terms

After you have completed your Master-List of Key Terms, quiz yourself. Go down the list and try to define or say something significant about each term on the list.

If possible, quiz yourself in private and describe, define, and discuss each term out loud, as if you were explaining it to someone else in the room. This procedure ensures that you take the time to explain each term fully. Many times, you look at a term, think you know it, and skip to the next one. However, you may not really be able to define the term as easily or as clearly as you think. By talking about each term, you see exactly how much you do or don't know about it. You also begin to feel more comfortable discussing these terms at length, which can help when you write an essay response.

Ultimately, you want to be able to go down the list and confidently define each term or say something about its significance. You probably won't be able to do that the first time. You might find yourself unable to remember a certain term or hesitating when you try to define or describe it in detail. There are several techniques you can use to learn these key words. You might, for example, simply go back to your original notes and read more about the key term you have difficulty remembering. However, if there are many terms that give you trouble, this can become a tedious and time-consuming process.

Instead of going back to your original notes each time you can't remember a term, you can create a more detailed Master-List of Key Terms that includes some brief definitions for certain terms. Divide this Master-List into two columns, with the terms in the left column and the brief definitions in the right. The first few times you quiz yourself on the list, you can look at both columns; seeing the brief definitions will trigger your memory. After doing this a few times, cover the right column and see how you do when you quiz yourself only looking at the key terms. If you get stuck, you can simply look at the right column to see the definition. Continue quizzing yourself this way until you no longer need to refer to the definitions at all.

The most effective way to memorize key terms is to work with cue cards. Cue cards are particularly helpful when you need to remember a great many key terms, such as new vocabulary words in a foreign language. Simply take 3×5 cards and write down a key term from the course on one side and either a definition or a description of its significance on the other.

Although making the cue cards might seem to be time consuming, this method has many advantages. First, the process of making the cards helps you begin to memorize the material. As you write down a term and its definition, your mind begins to process the information into your long-term memory. Second, using the cards enables you to shuffle and reorganize them in various ways. For example, you can eliminate cards for terms that you know very well, and continue to test yourself on the ones you don't.

Third, cue cards enable you to quiz yourself both ways; you can look at the term and test yourself on the definition or look at the definition and guess the term. If you can do both, then you truly know the term. This can particularly help you on those questions when you need to furnish the term yourself, such as fill-in-the-blank questions for which you are not given choices. For this reason, cue cards are particularly useful in preparing for foreign language exams that test you on new vocabulary words; on those exams, you sometimes need to know the English definition of a word and sometimes the foreign word in order to answer questions.

Be able to define and/or say something significant about each term on the Master-List of Key Terms. You can use cue cards or other memory techniques to help you learn them.

Cue cards make it very easy for you to test yourself on key terms. Sit with the stack of cards and, for each one, state the definition or description of the term. Then flip the card over to see if you were correct. If you were right and feel pretty confident that you won't forget the term, you can put the card aside. If you got it wrong or had trouble describing it in detail, put the card at the back of the stack. Before you do, though, read over the card a few times and make a concentrated effort to remember it. You won't be able to remember something merely because you've read it; you have to make an effort and instruct yourself to remember it. When you have finished going through the whole stack, take up the pile of "misses," shuffle it, and start again. Repeat the process, continuing to eliminate any cards you find you now know quite well. (If you continue to have trouble with some terms, you can then try to use some of the memory tips listed in Chapter 5.) Eventually you should be able to go through the whole deck and define each term without hesitation. You'll know then that you are ready for the exam.

You won't necessarily be able to go through the whole deck of cue cards successfully in your first sitting. However, that should not concern you. In fact, it's a good idea to work with the cards repeatedly; the more times you practice with the cards, the more likely you'll be able to remember the information on the exam. Try to quiz yourself with the cards several times over the course of several days preceding an exam. One advantage to using cue cards is that you can carry them around with you and quiz yourself at anyplace or anytime, even if you are waiting for a bus or during a commercial break while watching television. This will help you make efficient use of your study time before an exam; no free minute has to go to waste.

Even if you use cue cards, you should still make a Master-List of Key Terms on one sheet that you can quickly read over it at a glance. And in addition to using cue cards, there is a variety of other techniques for improving your memory you can use. They are described in more detail in Chapter 5.

As a final test before an exam, sit down with a blank sheet of paper and try to write down as many key terms from the course as you can remember. If you can recall almost all of the terms and what they mean, you are more than ready to go to the exam.

Working with the Master-List of General Themes and Topics

As was mentioned, you can first look closely at your Master-List of General Themes and Topics to determine the most important subjects and points that were covered in the course. You'll want to particularly focus your studying on these topics, especially the ones that recurred throughout a course. For example, knowing key terms that relate to these topics is probably more important than knowing a key term that came up only once and was not connected to a larger topic.

The Master-List of General Themes and Topics is also instrumental in helping you prepare for essay tests. When you take an essay examination in class, you are pressed for time. That's why many essay responses are messy and unorganized. It's hard, after all, to come up with a detailed, focused response right on the spot.

However, you've got your Master-List of General Themes, which provides you with clues as to possible essay questions before the test. You can examine the list and try to think about possible essay questions involving each theme. You can then take the time to plan answers to these questions *before* the exam.

You don't, however, have to write an elaborate practice essay for each theme or possible question you come up with. Instead, write down each general theme on a separate piece of paper. For each one, think about how you would approach an essay question related to that theme and make a list of the specific points, topics, and ideas you would incorporate into your response. If there are any key terms that also relate to the theme, list those as well.

Several times before the exam, sit down with these sheets and, using the list of points you've written for each theme, talk your way through the essay response you would write on the exam. You don't need to write out an elaborate response for each one unless you want to. By talking out loud, you begin to feel more and more comfortable discussing these themes. You should try to do this exercise at least twice for

> Use the Master List of General Themes and Topics to help determine your study strategy and to brainstorm possible essay questions.

each theme — once, looking at the detailed list of points you've created and once, looking at only the theme. If you can talk comfortably and at length about a general theme, you can also write an essay about it on an exam.

Of course, there's no guarantee that essay questions on the exam will reflect these themes in their original form. However, since most essay questions address broad topics, they will usually connect in some way with a general theme or themes. When you see the essay question, you can identify whichever theme(s) it relates to, and draw on the same concepts and points you previously thought about in conjunction with that general theme as you write your essay.

Working with the Master-List of Related Concepts

In preparing this complex list, you have already begun to learn from and apply it. By looking for the different groups of concepts from the course and identifying how they are related, you have reconceptualized your notes. Being able to rethink and reorganize different concepts indicates you have attained a certain degree of comfort and familiarity with these ideas.

The process of creating the Master-List has already involved a great deal of thought and effort. Now that you've done the hard part, all you need to do with this list

> Be comfortable with — and keep developing — your Master-List of Related Concepts.

is read it over a few times before the exam to keep these ideas fresh in your mind. Making this list in advance means you've already done some serious thinking about these ideas, more than most students do before taking a major exam. You can enter an exam feeling confident about your ability to examine, think about, and answer complicated questions.

At the same time, feel free to add to and continue to develop this list. In the process of preparing for an upcoming test, more related concepts might occur to you. Or, you might hit upon terms and topics that you can add to specific subject categories you've already placed on the list. The more ways you can find to connect terms, topics, and concepts together in new ways, the more variations of possible exam questions you anticipate.

Brainstorm Your Own Exam Questions

After you have gone over and quizzed yourself several times on the Master-Lists and feel pretty comfortable with them, you can start to brainstorm exam questions. Looking at the lists, try to write as many questions as you can. You can use the lists to create specific questions based on specific terms, topics and related concepts. You can also try to brainstorm questions that are not so specifically tied to items on the lists.

If you know the format for the exam, concentrate on writing the same kinds of questions as will be on the exam. If you do not know the exact format, write as many different types of questions as you can. In fact, even if you do know the format, as an exercise you can write questions for that format as well as for other types of questions. The act of writing questions in a variety of formats is one way to reorganize and reconceptualize information; it can help you better learn and retain information from the course.

Make it a goal to write some questions that are the most difficult questions you can imagine — even harder than the toughest teacher in the world would dare ask. If you can foresee and answer such difficult questions, you'll be able to breeze through the easy ones.

You might get lucky and get to the final exam to discover that you've foreseen many of the questions. If not, the questions most likely will be similar to those you've written. And if they are not similar, you haven't lost anything. Again, the act of brainstorming and writing questions is an active study technique that helps you become more familiar and comfortable with a particular subject.

As a final exercise, wait a day or two and then take your own exam. How many of your questions can you answer? You should be able to answer all of them. For any

Brainstorm and write your own test questions. Write the same type of questions as will be on your upcoming exam — as well as a variety of other types. Then take the test you wrote yourself. See if there are any areas that you need to study in more detail or get some help with.

that you get wrong, take more time to study the term, topic, or concept that relates to the question. If necessary, go back and reread your notes, or get help from the sources discussed in the next chapter.

Test Training Step 3:

Get Help When You Need It

Step 1: Reread and Reorganize Your Notes:
— Reread All Notes from Lectures and Readings
— Create Three Master-Lists from Notes

Step 2: Work with the Master-Lists
— Master-Lists and Exam Questions
— Quiz Yourself
— Brainstorm Your Own Exam Questions

Step 3: Get Help When You Need It

As you go about the first steps in preparing for an upcoming exam, you might discover you are uncertain, confused, or do not remember enough about a particular term or topic. Do not skip over it and assume it won't matter for the exam. Instead, you can get extra help from a variety of other sources discussed in this chapter so that by the time the exam comes, you will truly know about

> Don't overlook terms or points that confuse you or that you do not remember well — especially those that seem particularly important to the subject. Keep a list of troublesome topics and lingering questions.

and understand everything that is important about that particular subject.

While preparing for the exam, you might consider keeping a separate master list of confusing or troublesome terms and topics or a list of lingering questions. As time permits before the exam, you can then turn to some of the following sources for additional information and help. Try to determine which terms and questions on your list are particularly significant and make certain you investigate those further. Any others you can explore as time permits.

As you consult other sources, be sure to take additional notes on what you discover. You can then add to your Master-Lists based on the new information you track down.

Here are some sources you can consult for help and additional information:

See the Professor

When they sit down to study for a major exam, many students become confused or generally anxious about the test. In need of advice, they turn to what seems to be the most accessible

If you ask a professor or teacher for extra help, be prepared with specific questions. That way, you'll get specific answers.

and most reliable source of information — the professor. However, if you go to see a professor a few days before an exam and say, "I'm confused. I really need help. What do I do?" there's not all that much she can do for you this late in the game. Instead, if you come with a specific question, you can get specific information. If, as you are studying your notes, you come across anything that really confuses you, write down specific questions on a sheet of paper. Bring that sheet with you when you go to see the professor and go over the questions. In addition to providing you with information you need, the professor might also offer additional hints as to the content of the upcoming exam.

It is also important that you don't rely solely on the professor as your source of help. Once the semester is over, many professors become scarce, which makes it difficult to see them just before a final exam. If you wait to begin studying until after the course has ended, you may not get an opportunity to see the professor. Even if a professor schedules office hours before an exam, there's no guarantee you'll get in to see her. After all, many other students probably have the same idea. Try your best, if you need to, to track down the professor. If you can't, though, there are other ways to get help.

Read Other Sources

As you go over your notes and prepare the Master-Lists, you may come across terms or ideas that you don't understand, and you may find that even in your original classroom notes, you do not have clear enough information. Some of your required reading assignments may be especially difficult or poorly written. You also may find that, as time has passed, you have forgotten important information.

Fortunately, you can seek out and consult other reading materials for more comprehensive and understandable information. Even if you are not confused about a particular point, it's a good idea to read some additional sources anyway. The more sources you read about a particular subject, the more information you receive about it. And by reading about a subject in depth just before an exam, you immerse yourself in the material; you then enter the examination focused on and comfortable with that subject.

In the library, there are many reference materials that compile tremendous amounts of factual information about specific subjects, including academic encyclopedias and dictionaries for subjects of all kinds. These sources will likely include listings for many of the key terms you've studied in class, and they'll be easy to track down. By consulting these sources, you can easily find clear and concise explanations of these points. Go to the reference section of the library and ask the librarian to suggest reference sources for specific subjects.

You also might consult other textbooks on the same subject as your course. They probably cover the same terms and topics as your assigned textbook, but they might be described more clearly or in more detail. You can see if there are textbooks for your class in the reference section of the library, or go to the school bookstore and scan the books that are used for the same department as the one offering your current course.

There are also many published study guides for specific subjects that present clear, concise descriptions, explanations, and notes. These guides are by no means meant to replace the experience of going to class and reading assignments yourself. However, they can supplement your notes. You can refer to them for additional information about terms and other major topics in a particular subject, or to confirm your understanding of what a particular term means. You can go to a bookstore and scan the books in the study guide section to see if any relate to your course.

Consulting introductions to different editions of important primary texts can provide you with a great deal of additional information. For example, an introduction to a particular work of literature will often summarize the plot, describe the characters, and discuss major thematic and critical issues. Reading these introductions therefore helps you recall the work of literature in more detail, while providing additional points and ideas you might not have previously considered. You can also look for anthologies and collections that include articles and essays on a particular subject or by a certain writer. For example, an introduction to a volume of *Freud's Collected Writings* might

You can consult a variety of supplemental reading materials for additional information. It helps if you start preparing for an exam early on; that way, you leave yourself time for additional research.

summarize his major innovations, as well as critical reactions to and controversies surrounding them.

Reading about the same topic in several sources is a worthwhile exercise as it shows you how the same subject can be described in different ways. This is important because examination questions will often be worded in a manner different from the way the material was originally described to you.

Other sources can also provide a variety of examples and illustrations of major principles. The more examples you read, the better you understand the idea or principle behind them. Finding additional examples can be particularly helpful in preparing for math and science examinations for which you are asked to solve various problems using different formulas. Seeing a variety of sample problems before an exam makes you better prepared; you are able to see the many different problems that relate to a particular formula or principle. You can even find sources with sample problems and solutions so that you can practice questions before the exam.

For all these reasons, consulting with and reading additional sources are valuable study techniques in the days prior to an examination. Your priority, however, is creating

CHECKLIST OF OTHER READING SOURCES TO CONSULT

- Academic Encyclopedias and Dictionaries. You can consult general ones such as the *Encyclopedia Americana* or *Encyclopedia Britannica*, or those for specific subjects, such as arts and humanities, world and U.S. history, science and technology. Ask the reference librarian for suggestions.

- Introductions to various editions of a particular text, such as a work of literature, or collections and anthologies of works on specific subjects and/or by specific writers.

- Additional textbooks on the same subject (remember to check the index and table of contents to find sections you want to read).

- Additional books or articles on the same subject. For suggestions, check:

  — the bibliography or list of works cited in your textbook.
  — the subject catalog in the library.
  — the section of the library or bookstore where books on that subject are shelved.

- Study guides on different subjects specifically written for college students. Just be certain you only use these books to supplement your own notes, not in place of them.

and working with the three Master-Lists. If you have additional time during your study preparation period, you can then read other sources.

Work with Study Partners or Groups

In preparing for an examination, many students decide to work with a partner or to form a study group. As with consulting other sources, you might find other students have more detailed notes on particular topics or terms that can supplement your own. But this means of studying is not for everyone. Before deciding whether or not a study group would be helpful to you, consider the following advantages and disadvantages:

Advantages

- When you get together with other students, you have the opportunity to learn from one another. One student, for example, may have better notes or a better grasp of a particular subject than you do. You can use the other students as a source of information to flesh out certain points in your own notes.

- Answering questions that your fellow students have for you will also help you to study. Talking about a particular topic is an excellent way to gain familiarity with the material. In the process of describing and explaining a concept to someone else, you come to a better understanding of it yourself.

> If you are considering working with a study group, carefully consider the advantages and disadvantages. Choose your study partners carefully and make certain everyone gives and takes equally from the group study sessions.

- Being part of a study group ensures you study a certain amount of time before an exam; the group keeps you on a set study schedule. If you have difficulty motivating yourself to study, being part of a study group can give you the jump-start you need.

- Perhaps most importantly, being part of a study group provides emotional support during a difficult time. Studying for and taking exams is an extremely stressful, emotionally draining experience, especially if you feel you are alone. Meeting regularly with friends and peers going through the same experience can make you feel better. These meetings alleviate tension, as you laugh with your friends and help one another through the rough spots.

Disadvantages

- If the students in your study group have poor notes and don't really understand the subject matter themselves, you might spend all your time helping them and not receive any help in return. You particularly need to watch out for "study moochers" who haven't done any work all year and merely want to copy your notes.

- Panicky students are also a serious problem in a study group. There may be members who are so stressed out that instead of providing emotional support, they make you more nervous and worried about an exam than you were before. Additionally, the bulk of the study group's time may be spent trying to calm this one person down or discussing only those concepts he or she doesn't understand.

- Study groups often don't use available time efficiently. You may spend several hours with a study group and find you've only covered a small portion of material, much less than you could have studied on your own. There are several reasons why this might occur. Whenever a group of students get together, there is going to be a certain amount of chatting, joking, and socializing taking place, which takes up time. Another problem is that a large portion of time might be spent discussing some point you already know and understand perfectly. The time you spend going over that point might have been better spent studying something you still don't understand.

If you decide to find a partner or study group, be aware that choosing the right people to work with is the way to avoid some major disadvantages. A good study group involves give and take among all members; all members should be willing to work and should have something valuable to contribute to the group. It's also a good idea to limit the number of members in the group; any more than

> Being in a study group is no guarantee of study success.

five is probably going to waste more time and be more trouble than it's worth. At the same time, if you feel you work better on your own than in a group, don't feel that you are at any disadvantage.

Attend Review Sessions

Professors occasionally organize formal review sessions prior to an examination. At these study sessions, the professor or a teaching assistant will be available to answer questions regarding material from the course. You should make certain you attend these study sessions, even if you don't necessarily have a question yourself. You never know what kinds of hints a professor or teaching assistant might give about what will be on the test. It's also helpful to hear someone professional describing major concepts and key terms in their own words, as the examination questions may reflect the same language and phrasing. You can also try to use some of the same phrases and terminology in your essay responses.

Be cautioned, though, that these sessions tend to attract panicky students who use the time to voice their own fears and anxieties about the exam. In addition to wasting time in the session, these students can also make you begin to feel

If a review session is offered, it is worth it to go. Look for any special clues or hints about what is important to study for the exam. Avoid or ignore the panicky students.

stressed out yourself. Do your best to ignore them. The only person you need to listen to at the review session is the professor or teaching assistant. Another problem that might arise is that one or two students dominate the entire study session with their questions. If you have your own question, try to ask it right at the beginning of the session so that you guarantee you'll be heard.

Don't Forget:
Special Tips for
Improving Your Memory

A great deal of test preparation involves memorization, especially of key terms that are new to you, as you'll need to know that information to help you answer questions. In Chapter 3, you saw some suggestions for working with and reviewing key terms in a way that can help you retain the information (such as using cue cards). This chapter outlines a variety of additional tips to help improve your memory. You can use them to study for a test, or for any situation in which you need to remember something (such as learning people's names at a conference or meeting).

Why Is It Tough to Remember Things?

A very small percentage of people are gifted with photographic memories. They can read a passage of a text and then repeat it word for word from memory. Most of us, though, have a great deal of difficulty memorizing information. Like listening or reading, memorizing takes effort. To work on improving your memory, it helps to understand exactly how our memories work.

Psychologists and scientists believe there are two different levels of memory — short-term and long-term memory. Our short-term memory can "store" several items of new information that we have just been exposed to. Items stored in short-term memory are very easy to remember, since we've usually just learned them or been exposed to them. However, they also can only be stored for a very brief period of time and then we forget them. If we didn't, then our minds would be filled with absolutely pointless information that we'll never really use. For example, when you look at a phone number in the phone book, you can remember it for a few minutes — just enough time for you to use it — and then you'll usually forget it. At the same time, though, for certain phone numbers we use all the time, we are able to remember them. That's because they've become part of our long-term memory.

Some of what is "entered" into our short-term memory is transferred over to our long-term memory. The long-term memory can store much more information for longer periods of time. Anything that you are able to remember for long periods of time — whether it be scenes from favorite movies or information from school classes — has been stored in your long-term memory. The trouble is that the long-term memory stores so much information, it can be much more difficult to access the information. In many ways, your long-term memory is like a walk-in closet. You can keep stuffing more and more into it, but the more there is, the harder it becomes to get to the item you want.

General Tips for Improving Your Memory

Many students, in trying to memorize information for exams, fail to consider these aspects of how memory really works. They arrive at the exam, only to find that despite spending hours staring at lists of key terms, theories, and formulas, they are able to recall very little.

When you are studying for an exam, you want information to be stored in your long-term memory AND you want to be able to access it easily. After all, you'll probably need to remember a lot more than six or seven items, and for a longer period of time than a few minutes. At the same time, you'll want to be able to use what you've studied and memorized quickly, without having to wrack your brain trying to remember something you know you've studied.

You therefore have to devote a portion of your test preparation period to working at memorization. That means studying certain pieces of information a special way with the goal of being able to remember them later. It also means creating ways to help you remember the information quickly during an exam. To accomplish those goals, keep these general guidelines in mind:

Make an Active Effort to Remember

Studies have shown that to transfer information from the short-term to the long-term memory, you need to make a conscious effort to learn information with the goal of remembering it later; in other words, you need to make memorization an active process. The transfer won't take place automatically. That's why just reading your assignments or staring at lists of key words without doing something active won't really help you remember information for the test. You need to set up times specifically to work at memorizing.

Of course, you don't need to — nor should you attempt to — memorize all of your lecture notes and reading assignments; that would be far too time-consuming and virtually impossible to do. As we've seen earlier in this book, much of your work as a student, not only before an exam but throughout the semester, involves learning and coming to understand new ideas. By attending lectures and doing reading assignments, you come to some overall understanding of various concepts related to a particular subject. Your overall understanding of a particular subject will certainly be a factor in how well you do on an exam. However, in most of your classes and reading assignments, you'll also be exposed to specific pieces of information that you simply must commit to memory to use them — on homework assignments, in labs, on problem sets, and on examinations.

As you prepare for the exam, you should create some kind of list of items to be memorized. If you've been following the study guidelines outlined here, then you've done exactly that by creating your Master-List of Key Terms. You now need to spend time working actively, not only to read over but to memorize the information for the exam.

In addition to making this initial effort to memorize information, you need to take the time to "rehearse" repeatedly. Rehearsing means testing yourself over and over again to see what items you've tried to memorize you can actually recall. Any item you forget, you must again make the conscious effort to memorize. You should keep going over the items you are attempting to memorize again and again, testing yourself to see what you remember, until all of the information has made the transfer into your long-term memory.

Learn to Overlearn

Studies show that people who "overlearn" have a much easier time remembering what they've studied than people who are satisfied making only a few efforts to memorize a list of items. Overlearning means you do not stop studying and "rehearsing" the first time you successfully test yourself and are able to remember all the information you've been studying. Instead, you should keep on going over the information until you can remember the entire list of items several times. At that point, you will probably be sick of quizzing yourself, which is actually a good thing. It means you've successfully memorized the information and have improved your chances of recalling it later on.

Studies also show that the more times you expose yourself to material over a longer period of time, the more ingrained it becomes in your long-term memory. In fact, if you study a list of items and forget it later on, the next time

> Expose yourself repeatedly and over long stretches of time to information you are attempting to memorize, rather than in a single block of time.

you study the list, it will take less time to learn it and you'll be more likely to remember it. So, if you want to make certain you will remember information later, you should look at and think about it repeatedly over the course of several days. You'll have the time, then, to relearn anything you've forgotten, and what you've relearned you probably won't forget again.

You are much better off studying a list of key terms you want to memorize for an hour each day for five days than studying it for five hours on one day. By looking at the list every day, you train yourself to retrieve that information from your memory even after some time has passed. You'll probably find you get better at remembering the information as the week passes; you'll also begin to retrieve the information from your memory faster and with less effort.

Figure out Retrieval Cues

Even if you work actively to study lots of information, it can be tough to access it once you're in an exam. You might experience the "tip of your tongue" sensation, when you know that you know some piece of information but just can't seem to spit it out. To help access facts from your long-term memory, you can use "retrieval cues." These are words and images that are linked to other pieces of information you've memorized. By thinking about the retrieval cue, you then trigger your memory about the other information. Sometimes this happens automatically; for example, a particular smell will often trigger related memories, perhaps of a time or place when you had smelled smelled something similar. At the same time, you can work to create your own retrieval cues that will help you access knowledge quickly. You'll read about some of those techniques later in the chapter, in the section on mnemonics.

Understanding how retrieval from memory works can generally help you when you find yourself in a jam on an exam. Very often, you might find you can't remember some piece of information that you know you've studied. If you take a few minutes to think about other, related items you studied at the same time, you may find you successfully trigger your memory of the item you thought you'd forgotten. For example, if you've forgotten the chemical compound for hydrochloric acid, you might think about other compounds you studied that you are able to remember and see if they spark any additional memories.

You can also try recreating your initial effort to learn and memorize the material. Perhaps your memory of the entire experience will help trigger memories of specific pieces of information. Close your eyes and try to visualize yourself as you were when first studying the information. What were you wearing? Where were you sitting? Were there distinctive sights or smells in the room? See if you can, in your mind, picture the piece of paper with the information on it. Can you see what's written? Can you possibly see the information you're trying to remember? Even if you can't "see" the information this way, just thinking about the entire scene may help you successfully retrieve more information.

Of course, you should not spend much time trying to recall information in this manner. If you really can't access the information, move on to other portions of the exam. Sometimes the best way to remember something is not to try so hard. You might find the information suddenly pops into your head later on, even though you are working on something completely different.

Organize Information

If you study information in an organized manner that makes logical sense, you'll also find you have an easier time remembering it later.

Studies indicate that people who organize information for themselves and then attempt to memorize it remember much more than people who try to memorize random, unrelated lists of items. That means that as you prepare lists and attempt to memorize them, you should group items in smaller categories that logically belong together. For example, if you have an enormous list of key terms from a course, rather than going down the list and trying to memorize it all, regroup similar items into categories. You might, for example, group names of important people together and study them separately from other items, such as dates and historical events. Similarly, if you're studying for a vocabulary test in a foreign language, you might group verbs separately from nouns. The categories you choose to create are up to you, provided they make some kind of logical sense.

Sleep On It

Believe it or not, one thing you can do to help improve your memory is sleep. Studies have shown that you are more likely to remember something you've read just before going to bed. While you are asleep, your mind processes the information, moving it into your long-term memory. There's no guarantee that studying just before going to sleep is going to be more effective for you than studying at other times during the day; however, it is certainly worth trying. Reading over the Master-List of Key Terms right before you go to sleep; when you wake up the next morning, quiz yourself and see how much you remember. At the very least, studying the list each night for several nights before an exam ensures you expose yourself to the material repeatedly throughout your study period.

Mnemonic Devices to the Rescue

In addition to the general strategies described above, you can use specific *mnemonic devices* to help you remember various items of information for an exam. A mnemonic device is any strategy that helps improve memory of specific items. By working to come up with a mnemonic device, like the ones listed here, you ensure you work actively to memorize and transfer information to long-term memory.

Many of the mnemonic devices listed here also provide retrieval cues, helping you access information more easily when you need it during an exam.

Here are some mnemonic devices and other strategies that can help you memorize information — and easily recall what you've memorized later on:

Write It Down

Writing is an active process that can help you move information into your long-term memory. In taking notes and reworking them into Master-Lists using the strategies discussed earlier, you are of course writing down information. This activity is an active learning process that can help you remember. However, if you want extra help remembering certain terms and other important information, you can write even more. You can try, for example, writing a term and its definition several times. Study what you write as you do it, to provide extra concentration. After a few times of copying what you see, try to write the same word and definition without help; put away the notes or close your eyes and try to write down what you remember. Wait a few hours and then try writing the term and definition again. Were you able to remember them?

Cue Cards

As we discussed earlier, you can make cue cards to help you memorize information. Just by making the cards — which involves writing a term on one side and information about it on the other — you begin working to learn and memo-

> Writing about something can help you better memorize it. Studying just before going to sleep might also help you retain information.

rize the information. You can then "rehearse" the information by quizzing yourself on the cards. To make certain you "overlearn" the information, don't eliminate cards from the pile until you've gotten them correct several times. You should also make certain you run through your stack of cards a few times a day for several days before an upcoming exam. Again, that ensures you have overlearned and means you'll more likely remember the information — and cut down on the time and effort of retrieving it.

By the way, you can continue using writing to help you learn facts from your cue cards. If, while quizzing yourself, you miss a term, you can write it at least two more times on a piece of paper before quizzing yourself again. The repetitive writing is one way to make an active effort to learn the information. You can also try using any variety of mnemonic devices listed here.

Rhymes

Ancient storytellers who didn't know how to read or write could recite epic-length poems completely from memory. The trick they used was to depend on rhythm, alliteration, and especially rhyming words to help trigger their memories of the entire work. For example, if they could remember the first line of a rhymed couplet, the second one would easily come to mind; similarly, if they could remember the rhyming words that ended each couplet, they could usually recall the lines in their entirety.

Since then, many people have used short rhymes to help them remember various facts. Some of the more well-known rhymes used for mnemonic purposes are "In 1492, Columbus sailed the ocean blue" and "Thirty days hath September, April, June, and November." You can create your own rhymes to help you remember information about key terms for an exam. Try to find some word that rhymes with the term and write a short phrase or sentence that connects the two. For example, if you want to remember what a mnemonic device is, you might remember this short rhyme: "Use a mnemonic device so you won't forget twice."

Some terms lend themselves more easily to rhymes than others; if you can't come up with a rhyme relatively quickly, then you should probably try some other device so that you don't waste much study time.

Alliterative Clauses

Alliterative clauses are simply phrases in which each word begins with the same letter or sound, such as "King Kong" or "Peter Piper picked a peck of peppers." You can use alliteration as a mnemonic device. Take whatever key term you are trying to memorize and see if you can find some word that begins with the same letter that will trigger more detailed information about the term.

For example, the word "plethora," according to the dictionary, means "excess" or "abundance." You can, though,

> Use mnemonic devices to help you improve your memory. Mnemonic devices include rhymes, alliterative clauses, mental associations, visualizations, and acronyms.

associate "plethora" with "plenty." Since both plethora and plenty begin with the letter "p" (in fact, they both begin with the sound "pl"), it's much easier to remember the word "plenty" than "abundance." The word plenty, though, makes you think of having too much of something; in other words, an abundance.

As the above example indicates, you can use alliteration to help you remember definitions of terms. You can also use it to help you retrieve any information associated with a particular term that you need to know. For example, if you need to remember that a "synapse" is part of the nervous system, you could link "synapse" to the word "senses," which in turn would remind you of the nervous system which affects our senses of pain, pleasure, etc. If you want to be more specific and remember that a synapse is the gap between neurons, you can also use alliteration. For example, you might link "synapse" to "space." Both begin with the letter "s." In fact, you could become even more specific and use link the word "synapse" to "sinus," which both begin with a similar sound ("si" or "sy"). A sinus is also an empty space, which can therefore help you think of a gap. Thus when you think of the word "synapse," it is linked easily by alliteration to the word sinus, which then leads you to picture and remember that it is a gap.

Associations

One way to remember information about a term is to find a word (or image) you associate with the term that you link with another piece of information you need to remember about it (such as a definition, or some related piece of important information). This mental association functions as a link; by remembering the mental image, you easily remember both the term and the more detailed information associated with it.

For example, if you want to remember that Edison created the lightbulb, you can look at Edison's name and see the word "son" in it. "Son" sounds just like "sun," so you can associate Edison's name with the sun. The sun, of course, is a source of light. So, by linking Edison with the sun, you can then bring to mind the image of light and the lightbulb.

Similarly, if you wanted to remember that Marconi invented the telegraph, you could stare at Marconi's name and see that it is similar to the word "macaroni." When you think of macaroni, you think of long strings of pasta. When you think of long strings, you think of telegraph wires. Therefore, you can link Marconi to telegraph wires with the image of macaroni.

When you try to create these mental associations, it's often helpful to rely on your personal experiences. For example, one student who needed to remember that John Keats wrote "Ode on a Grecian Urn" thought of her Uncle John who had visited Greece the previous summer. By linking "John" and "Greece" in her mind, she was able to remember that John Keats wrote the poem about the Grecian urn.

You can get as creative as you need to be in finding these associations. If necessary, you can think up a detailed, elaborate story that will help you link a word with information about it. And it can be as silly, illogical, or personal as you like, just so long as it works. A mental association only needs to make sense to you. You don't have to feel obliged to share it with other people.

Visualizations

You've probably heard the expression "A picture paints a thousand words." Well, it's also much easier to remember pictures than words. You can therefore use mental images and pictures instead of words and phrases to help you remember something. For example, one way to associate two or more words is to create a picture in your mind in which they are connected. If you want to remember that John Keats wrote "Ode to a Grecian Urn," for example, you might picture such an urn filled with enormous keys (which sounds like "Keats") inside of it.

Visualizations can particularly help you remember and associate several different terms or images. If you want, for example, to remember that the Department of Agriculture is part of the president's cabinet, you can picture a stalk of corn inside of a large, oak cabinet. You can then add to that mental image by placing other objects in the cabinet to indicate other departments in the president's cabinet, such as a giant penny to indicate the treasury, a gun to indicate the defense, and a set of scales to indicate justice.

You can also use visualizations to remember lists of items in some kind of order or hierarchy. First, you create a visual image for each item on the list; then you find ways to link those images. For example, if you wanted to remember the states in alphabetical order, you first could create visual images associated with each one.

Alabama:	*An alligator (to convey the "ala" sound at the start of the word)*
Alaska:	*An igloo (an image usually associated with Alaska)*
Arizona:	*A cactus in the endzone of a football field (to give you an image of an "arid" "zone")*
Arkansas:	*Noah's ark (for the ark sound)*

Next, you simply tie the images together in a larger visualization. You could, for example, picture the items piled on top of one another; you start with an alligator with an igloo on his head, on top of which is a goal post with a cactus beneath it, on which is perched Noah's ark, etc.

Another method people use to visualize items in order is to "place" them in some kind of space. For example, you might need to remember items within a hierarchy, in which each item is subservient to or of lesser value than the one above it. To remember the hierarchy, you could picture various levels of a building, and put visual items tied to key words on different levels. To remember the items in order, you just visualize the building, picturing yourself touring it from floor to floor. As you "see" items on each level, you'll remember which items are higher up than others.

For example, the major categories of living organisms follow this hierarchy:

Kingdom
    Phylum
        Class
            Order
                Family
                    Genus
                        Species

To remember them in order, you first need to link each to an image or word:

Kingdom: *Crown (for "King")*
Phylum: *Phone (for "Ph" sound in both words)*
Class: *A student's desk (for a school "class")*
Order: *A waitress (who takes "orders")*
Family: *A member of your family.*
Genus: *A pair of blue jeans (for the "gene" sound)*
Species: *A pair of spectacles (for the letters "spec")*

Now, you can imagine these items on various levels of a three-story house. On the roof of the house sits a crown. Inside the attic, beneath the roof, is an old phone. On the steps leading down from the attic is a student's desk. In the hallway by the upstairs bedrooms you see a waitress. As you start down the stairs to the first floor, you see a family member. Once downstairs, you see jeans strewn about. In the basement, you find a pair of spectacles.

As you mentally take this tour from top to bottom of the house, you'll then remember the hierarchy for the major groups. You'll know that "crown"/Kingdom are at the top of the list, while "phone"/Phylum is the next category down, and so on.

Acronyms

An acronym is a word that is formed by taking the first letters from several words in a series. They can be instrumental in helping you to remember a long list of items, especially if you need to remember the terms in a particular order.

For example, to remember the color spectrum, many students memorize the name "Roy G. Biv." This acronym is made by taking the first letter of each color in the spectrum order:

> *Red*
> *Orange*
> *Yellow*
> *Green*
> *Blue*
> *Indigo*
> *Violet*

Sometimes the first letters of a series of terms are not going to make a simple, easy-to-remember name like "Roy

G. Biv." In those cases, you can create a sentence where the first letter of each word corresponds to the first letter of the terms you are memorizing.

For example, to remember all of the planets in order, many students memorize the sentence: "My very earnest mother just served us nine pickles." The first letter of each word in that sentence corresponds to the first letter of a planet:

My	*Mercury*
Very	*Venus*
Earnest	*Earth*
Mother	*Mars*
Just	*Jupiter*
Served	*Saturn*
Us	*Uranus*
Nine	*Neptune*
Pickles	*Pluto*

Yes, it's a silly sentence. But time and time again, it does the trick. And that's all that matters.

Last-Minute Cram Sheets

Sometimes, no matter how hard you study, there are certain terms you will find extremely difficult to memorize. When all other methods fail, you can create a last-minute cram sheet for yourself. The night before an exam, take a single index card and write down any terms, facts, phrases or formulas you can't remember along with very brief definitions or explanations (they need to be brief so you can fit all of this information on a single index card). You especially want to include any terms you think will likely show up on an exam.

Take this card with you to the exam and arrive a few minutes early. Before the examination begins, you can stare at and study the card. (If you are allowed, you can sit at a desk in the exam room and study the card; if not, you can find a place to sit outside the room.) Continue to look at the card until the exam begins and you are asked to put away all of your notes. As soon as you receive your copy of the exam, before you look at a single question, write down everything you remember from the card in the margins of the examination booklet. Since you just looked at the card, the information on it should still be in your short-term memory, which means it should be easier for you to recall. You should be able to remember most of the information on the card for at least five minutes.

The cram card is a particularly effective tool for math and science exams for which you need to use formulas to solve problems and answer questions. You can write all the formulas on the card and read over it right before the exam. At the start of the exam, you can then write all of the formulas somewhere in the exam book and refer back to them throughout the test. Whenever you need to solve a problem or answer a question based on a particular formula, you can simply go back and glance at the formulas you wrote down. You won't have to struggle to remember them every time you have to answer a question.

If you bring a cram sheet with you to the exam, it is very, very important that you put the card away before the exam begins. You are usually free to examine your notes in

> As a last resort, you can use a last minute cram sheet to study from just before an exam. Be careful, though, that you do not break any rules that might be considered cheating; put it away before the exam starts, or consult it only before you enter the exam room.

the minutes before an exam starts. Once the examination officially begins and the proctor instructs you to put your books away, you cannot have any notes out. Don't put the card in your pocket or lay it beside your desk; instead, put it inside your book bag and put all of your books under your desk. You don't want the card anywhere in sight during an exam or you risk being accused of cheating. Even if you weren't actually looking at the card during an exam, a proctor might see it out in the open and assume you were. Don't take that risk. Make certain you put the cram card completely out of sight.

Test Your Memory Exercise

Imagine that you need to memorize the names of the first ten presidents of the United States in order of their terms in office. Study the following list using whatever mnemonic devices described you think will help. If you need help coming up with mnemonic devices, you can look at the suggestions on the following pages. Wait several hours, and try to list these presidents in order on a blank sheet of paper. How many could you remember? For those you forgot, re-examine your mnemonic device, or create a new one. Now try waiting twenty-four hours and quiz yourself again. How much can you now remember? How about after seventy-two hours?

The First Ten Presidents of the United States

George Washington
John Adams
Thomas Jefferson
James Madison
James Monroe
John Quincy Adams
Andrew Jackson
Martin Van Buren
William Henry Harrison
John Tyler

Mnemonic Device A

Visualizations: Create some kind of visual image for each of the presidents' names.

George Washington	*a pile of wash*
John Adams	*a basket of apples or an Adam's apple*
Thomas Jefferson	*a jar of Jif peanut butter (for Jeff, as in Jefferson)*
James Madison	*A Madison Avenue street sign*
James Monroe	*monkeys*

John Quincy Adams	*a quivering Gomez Addams*
Andrew Jackson	*jacks*
Martin Van Buren	*a van on fire (as in a van burning, similar to Van Buren)*
William Henry Harrison	*a furry sun in the sky (as in a hairy sun, close to Harrison)*
John Tyler	*someone putting down ceramic tiles in a shower stall (as in a "tiler")*

To distinguish further between Jefferson and Jackson, which both start with the same letter, you can pick a visual image that starts with the same two letters; for example, you might choose **je**ep for **Je**fferson, and **ja**cks for **Ja**ckson.

To memorize the presidents in order, you can now use these visualizations in a sequence. Picture each image piled on top of or somehow connected to the previous one, starting with the pile of wash for Washington.

> *On top of the pile of wash, you can picture a basket of apples.*
>
> *The tops of the apples are smeared with Jif peanut butter.*
>
> *Stuck in the peanut butter is a sign for Madison Avenue.*
>
> *Swinging from the Madison Avenue sign is a monkey.*
>
> *Holding onto the monkey is a quivering Gomez Addams.*
>
> *Gomez is throwing jacks into the air.*
>
> *The jacks are hitting the windshield of a burning van.*

The flames of the van are setting the hair of that hairy sun on fire.

A tiler is putting tiles all over the sun to control the flames.

Mnemonic Device B

Use acronyms to remember the order of the first ten presidents, using the first letter from each one's last name:

> *Washington*
> *Adams*
> *Jefferson*
> *Madison*
> *Monroe*
> *Adams*
> *Jackson*
> *Van Buren*
> *Harrison*
> *Tyler*

You can form several nonsense words from the first letter of each person's last name: Wajm Maj Vht (pronounced something like wahgem, mahg, viht).

Or you can try to create a sentence, with each word starting with the same letter as a president's last name: *W*hile *A*dam's *J*eep *M*oves *M*onkeys, *A*lice's *J*alopy *V*entures *H*igher *T*oo.

Yes, it is a silly sentence. But who cares? We're the only ones who need to know about it. And it will do the trick.

Word Power:

Special Tips for Improving Your Vocabulary

One of the keys to improving your performance on an exam is to improve your vocabulary. You might think you only need to study vocabulary for the SAT or for English and foreign language exams on which you are specifically tested on new words. However, as we've seen in earlier chapters, a great deal of the notes you take and need to memorize are lists of new terms for which you must know definitions. Virtually any new subject you study is going to introduce you to new terms with which you are unfamiliar. Rather than merely studying them, using them once and then forgetting them, you can work to make these terms part of your general vocabulary; that will make it much easier to recall and use them on an exam.

Additionally, by expanding your vocabulary you improve your chances for exam success in other ways. Many exam questions, regardless of the subject matter, will be

Improving your vocabulary can help you do better in school, particularly on exams. You might often encounter sophisticated new words on exam questions; knowing the word can help you answer the question correctly. You can also use these words when writing essays.

worded in a sophisticated, academic style that includes certain new words. Your teacher, who is writing the exam questions, is familiar with the more sophisticated terms used to discuss his or her chosen field. There's a good chance, therefore, that those words will somehow be incorporated into different exam questions.

At the same time, if you can incorporate more sophisticated words into your essays — whether they be term papers or examination essays — you will sound more intelligent and your teacher will likely be more impressed by your writing. It's therefore worth the time and effort to make it a habit to improve your overall vocabulary, and also to become familiar with the specific terms and words favored by those working in specific fields you are studying.

This chapter outlines several suggestions for improving your overall vocabulary. Improving your vocabulary involves several components. First, you have to seek out new words worth learning (unless you are specifically given words by your teacher, as is often the case with foreign language classes). Then, you need to make the effort to learn and memorize the words (for which you can use many of the strategies and mnemonic devices described in the previous chapter). Finally, you need to get in the habit of using the words so that you do not forget them. These various components are discussed in more detail in this chapter.

Discovering New Words

If you want to improve your vocabulary, you first need to identify new words to learn, memorize, and use. You could simply sit with a dictionary and go page by page, trying to memorize each word and its definition, but you'd be lucky to finish even the letter "A" within your lifetime. As we all know, there are certain words more commonly used than others. The ones most worth knowing are the ones you're most likely to encounter or use yourself — in conversation, in readings, in school, or at your job.

There are also certain words that are commonly used only in particular contexts and situations. In general, there are certain more sophisticated words commonly used in academia — words professors use in lecturing to their classes, in talking to one another about their professions, and in their own writing, as well as words you'll find in academic texts, such as textbooks and articles. These are the words you are often tested on for the SAT, because, while not used in most everyday conversation, they do tend to crop up in academic discussions and texts.

> Keep track of new words that you come across while reading or studying particular subjects, or going to classes.

When it comes to specific school subjects, you'll find there are certain words and terms that are favored by those working in those areas. When you read texts for those courses or listen to professors teaching those classes, you might start to hear these words over and over. Very often, the professors or authors will assume that you are as familiar with the term as they are, so they won't bother to provide you with the definition. You might just let the term slide by without bothering to find out its meaning; however, chances are you'll encounter it again — perhaps even on a test — and will wish you knew it. It's well worth it to you to become familiar with the "lingo" of whatever subject you are studying.

To narrow down your search for new words, then, you should begin compiling lists of these words as they come up in various contexts. To do that, you might consider keeping a special log book of new words. You can divide the book into sections — one big section for new words you encounter in general (such as in the newspaper, in conversation, or in pleasure reading), and separate sections for each course you are taking. As you come across new words, you can list them in the proper section.

In addition to finding words in your everyday reading and in your course work, you might consider some other sources for new words. There are several calendars on the market that provide you with a new word each day. You could purchase one and add those words to your log book. You also might try doing crossword puzzles, which are filled with interesting, sophisticated words.

To get you started, here's a list of vocabulary words that are often used in written academic works. You'll probably encounter these words in some of your reading assignments for school. You'll see that for each word, there's a concise definition and an example of the word used in a sentence, which, as is discussed later, is an important part of the learning process.

evince— to display clearly, show or reveal

> A detailed study of these two plays will *evince* many similarities between them.

formulate— to put into a set statement or expression, to devise (as in a policy or plan)

> The novel's theme is *formulated* in the final chapter.

fortuitous— lucky, happening by chance, accidental

> It was certainly *fortuitous* that they ran into each other in London.

germane— relevant, appropriate to, fitting

> A discussion of bone structure is certainly *germane* to our study of anatomy.

hegemony— those persons or institutions in power over others

> The church was a *hegemonic* institution in the Middle Ages.

heinous— shockingly evil and hateful

Richard III is the most *heinous* of Shakespeare's villains.

illuminate— to make clear, shed light on

This paper will *illuminate* the specific connections between the author's life and work.

ingenuous— showing innocent and child-like simplicity and candor; noble and honest, trusting

She is so *ingenuous*, she will trust just about anyone.

juxtapose— to place side by side for the sake of comparison

If we *juxtapose* a painting by Van Gogh with one by Matisse, their similar use of color becomes clear.

manifest— to make evident or certain by showing or displaying

His concern for the underprivileged has been made *manifest* many times by his extensive volunteer work.

ontological— relating to the nature of existence and our knowledge of it

Her writings have taken an *ontological* twist now that she has begun to discuss more personal issues.

perspicacity— acute mental power; shrewdness

Your adept performance in that oral examination demonstrated your *perspicacity*.

plethora— an abundance or excess

To prove my point, I will raise a *plethora* of sources and pieces of evidence.

praxis— customary action or practice

It is usually easier to understand something in *praxis* rather than theory.

preponderance— a majority; a superiority in power, importance, number, or strength

In the election, she has a *preponderance* of devoted followers.

prevalent— widespread; generally accepted, seen or favored

Signs that the economy is not doing well are certainly *prevalent.*

Learning New Words

In addition to compiling your lists of words, you need to make the effort to learn what they mean and memorize them; after all, lists of words that are meaningless won't really help you much. You can, if you like, look up words as soon as you initially see them and immediately copy them with their definitions into your log book. By doing this, you have the benefit of immediately seeing the word used in some context. Knowing a word's meaning will help make the rest of your reading more understandable.

However, looking up and memorizing every new word you encounter while you are trying to read is not always necessary, nor is it always helpful. Some words you encounter might be rather obscure and not worth the time and effort to memorize. If you wait until you complete an

> Make it a special point to look up definitions for new words that seem particularly important or are repeated. You can do this when you first encounter the word, or set aside time each week to go over a list of new words.

entire reading assignment, or several assignments, you can then see which words are repeated. Those are the ones well worth studying. (If you find you just cannot understand the reading without knowing what a particular word means, then look it up at that moment.)

At the same time, looking up words can slow down the reading process and detract from your ability to follow the flow of the argument. However, jotting down the word on a list only takes a second. So make it a practice to at least note the new words you encounter while reading. You can then return to your lists of words at some later point and begin looking up their definitions. You could look up all the words when you've completed a particular reading assignment, or you might set aside some time each week. Try to set a goal for yourself of learning a set number of new words each week, perhaps five to ten, and set aside a specific time to do so. You could then flip through your book and select the five to ten words that seem to have been the most important during your reading for that week and concentrate most on learning those words.

Each time you look up a new word, you should jot down a brief definition of it in your log book. However, you

> Write a brief definition of each word you look up, if possible use only one to three words.

do not need to copy the entire definition. Dictionary definitions can be quite wordy. You can usually jot down just two or three words that will convey the essential meaning of the word. For example, if you look up the word "superfluous," the definition reads, "exceeding what is sufficient or necessary; marked by wastefulness." You could simply note "excess; wasteful" and get the general sense of the word.

Additionally, the dictionary may list several definitions for a word, from the more prevalent to the more obscure. In most cases, only the prevalent meanings will be important; those are the ones you'll want to write down.

After writing down the definition of the word, you need to make the effort to memorize it, so you'll be able to use it later on. To do so, you can use these memorization strategies (discussed in detail in the previous chapter):

Cue Cards
Cue cards are an excellent way to memorize and test yourself on new words. Simply put the word on one side of an index card, and write its brief definition on the other. You then should spend time quizzing yourself on the stack of cards. Run through the cards looking at each word and then saying its definition out loud. For each one you get wrong, make a special effort to remember it (perhaps by repeating the word and its definition several times out loud, or writing it down

> Write several sentences using the word correctly in context.

several times, or creating a mnemonic device). You also should test yourself in reverse, looking at the definitions and trying to recall the words. Each time you successfully test yourself on a set of five to ten words, you can add the cards to the bigger stack containing all the new words you've been learning. Every once in a while, test yourself on the whole pile to see how many words you can remember.

Rhymes or Alliteration

It is much easier to remember a word's meaning if you can find definitions that rhyme with the word or share the same first few letters. For example, the definition of "paradigm" is "an outstandingly clear or typical example or pattern." You can simply remember that a "paradigm" is a "pattern," which starts with the same two letters. Similarly, you can remember the word "veracity" as meaning "honesty," as the "ty" ending makes them sound similar.

Visual Links

As we saw in the last chapter, a visual image can serve as the retrieval cue to help you easily access more detailed information. You can examine words or parts of words and create visual images that you associate with them and with the definition of the word.

For example, if you want to remember that the word "imperious" means arrogant or domineering, you could examine the word and focus on the word "imp" at the start of it. You could then picture a rather snobby "imp." In the future, when you see the word "imperious," you'll get a mental flash of that snobby imp, and thereby remember the definition.

Here's another example: "Perspicacious" means smart, keen, shrewd. The first several letters of the word — "perspi" — are the same as in the word "perspire." To learn what the word means, you can visualize someone on a TV quiz show perspiring beneath the hot lights — an image of a smart, "perspicacious" person that is linked with the word "perspire."

By the way, this method can be particularly helpful when you attempt to memorize definitions of words in a foreign language. Even though the original word is not in English, you can usually identify English words (or parts of words) within the foreign word and use them to create visual images. For example, in French, the word "lapin" means rabbit. You can see the English word "lap" in the French word, and then visualize a warm, cuddly rabbit nested in your lap.

Word Breakdown

As you study words, it can often be tremendously helpful to break them down into smaller parts. You can do this by identifying prefixes and suffixes. A prefix refers to word elements that are added to the beginning of certain words that change or enhance the meaning. Suffixes are added to the end of the words, and similarly add or change the word's meaning. For example, "mistrust" includes the prefix "mis" added to the word "trust." By placing the prefix "mis" in front of trust, you change the word, making it mean *not* to trust someone. Similarly, adding "ology" to certain words (or parts of words) indicates the "study of" some subject. For example, sociology is derived from a form of the word "society" and "ology."

There are certain common prefixes and suffixes with which you can become familiar. That way, whenever you see them, you can have some sense of what the word means, even if you don't know the word itself. That might help, for example, on exams; if you encounter words with which you are unfamiliar but do know the meaning of a prefix or suffix of the word, you may be able to gain a sense of the word's connotation. At the very least, it might help you figure out the gist of whatever question contains the word. Additionally, when you try to memorize words with familiar prefixes or suffixes, you don't have to work as hard, as you already know the meaning of part of it.

Here is a list of some common prefixes and suffixes. You can also start noting others you identify in your log book.

Use It or Lose It

Once you have successfully identified and memorized the definitions of new words, it is crucial that you begin to use them — and use them frequently. The more you use words,

PREFIXES

pre-   earlier than, prior to, before (as in preview and prewar)

post-   afterward, later (as in postgame show)

arch-   chief, principal (as in archenemy)

co-   joint, with, together (as in cocreator or cowriter)

neo-   new, newly formed, recent (as in neoimpressionism)

pseudo-   false, phony (as in pseudonym)

de-   do the opposite, reverse, remove, reduce (as in deemphasize)

mis-   wrongly, badly (as in misuse and misbehave)

dis-   do the opposite of, undo (as in disassociate and disavow)

sub-   under, beneath, below (as in subordinate and subpar)

proto-   first, beginning, giving rise to others (as in prototype)

non-   not, other than, reverse of (as in nonsense and nonabrasive)

SUFFIXES

-nomy   system of laws governing or sum of knowledge about (as in astronomy)

-ism   an act, practice, or process (as in criticism and plagiarism)

-ate   acted upon, marked by having, affected by (as in fortunate)

-ous   full of, filled with, abounding in (as in poisonous and treasonous) the more easily accessed they become. However, long periods of disuse means the words get lost somewhere in your long-term memory and they'll be harder to recall.

When you first write down a word's definition, you might want to immediately brainstorm and write down a few sentences that use the word. This will get you in the habit of actually using the word and help you become familiar with the contexts in which the word might come up. Next, try to use the word in conversation or your writing. This, of course, will be easier to do with some words than with others. However, you will probably have occasion to use many words you discover in doing your school assignments. You can use them when asking questions of your professor, in your homework assignments, and on essays and exams.

When and Where to Train for Tests

When to Study: Preparing Your Training Schedule

Just as athletes follow set regimens to help them train and be in prime condition for a game or competition, you need to create a strict training schedule for the period leading up to an exam — and make certain you follow it.

When planning your study schedule, you need to consider the number of exams you are going to be taking and the amount of time you have available before an exam to study. If you are preparing for only one exam and you have plenty of free time available to study, then you can be somewhat flexible in your schedule. Conversely, if you are studying for several exams in a brief time period, you need to create a strict schedule for yourself in which you devote certain hours each day to studying of specific subjects.

In general, you should avoid studying too soon before the exam because you want the material you've prepared to remain fresh in your mind. At the same time, you need

> Prepare a strict training regimen to help you prepare for an upcoming exam. Block out times for the stages in the training strategy outlined in earlier chapters.

enough time to go over your notes, prepare and work with the Master-Lists, brainstorm questions, and read additional sources and/or get help. To provide enough time to accomplish all this, you should begin studying for an exam at least five to seven days before the examination.

You can divide your study preparation into several stages. The first stage is to read through all of your notes from lectures and readings and create the Master-Lists. You should do this in one sitting, so make sure you designate a large enough block of time (probably about four to six hours for each course) at the beginning of your study preparation period.

Following the initial stage, the bulk of your study preparation should be devoted to working with the Master-Lists as described in earlier chapters — trying to memorize key terms, talking your way through lists of themes, topics, and concepts, and brainstorming possible questions. If you have the time, you can also read additional sources. Divide your day into blocks of time devoted to different tasks; you might, for example, spend the morning reading sources in the library, and the rest of the day and evening working with the Master-Lists.

If you are studying for more than one examination, make certain you only study a single subject at one time and give yourself a break of at least a half hour before you begin working on another course. You don't want to study several subjects all at once or within a short time frame because the material can easily become mixed together in your mind. Focusing on a single subject at a time helps you retain the information more effectively. Create a study schedule for yourself in which you divide your day into different study sessions with breaks in between. Devote each study session to preparing for a single examination.

During the week prior to a major examination, it is extremely important that you get plenty of sleep and eat well. Your mind is doing some hard work during this period, so let your body take a rest. You may feel you are getting a great deal accomplished by staying up late at night studying, but you are actually doing more harm than good. If you get overly tired, it becomes much more difficult to retrieve information from your long-term memory. If you arrive at an examination feeling exhausted, you won't be able to work through problems with a clear head.

The night before a major exam, you should give yourself a break and take it easy. However, that doesn't mean you should necessarily take the whole night off. It's fine to read over the Master-Lists one final time to keep all of the information fresh in your mind. When you've done that

If preparing for more than one exam, give yourself some time off between studying individual subjects.

successfully, then watch TV or go to a movie. And make certain you get a good night's sleep.

If You Do Cram

The most effective way to study is to give yourself several days, or ideally a week, in which to prepare. Of course, not everyone is able to do that all the time. If you do find yourself having to cram and study the day or night before a major test, do it wisely. The worst thing you can do is to pull an "all-nighter," drinking loads of caffeine to keep you awake. Even if you cover a great deal of material in those hours, you'll be so exhausted the next day you won't have the stamina to make it through the exam. You may know the material, but you won't have the energy to write a detailed essay, and your mind will be so foggy, you won't remember what you did study. You can cram, but make certain you get at least four hours of sleep. The time spent resting will be more helpful to you than if you stayed up reading and studying all night.

The smart way to cram is to read through all of your notes from class and reading assignments. But instead of making three Master-Lists, you can make one on which you list only those terms, themes, or concepts that you don't necessarily have a grasp on. If you have the time, try to read through all of your notes twice; although you won't have the time to think through and memorize everything from

Try not to get in a situation where you have to cram.
If you must, do it wisely. Don't stay up all night.

the Master-Lists, reading through all your notes twice will
at least expose you to the material. Another strategy is to
take educated guesses and study only subjects, topics, and
terms that seem likely to turn up on an exam. Of course,
this involves taking a gamble, but it might pay off.

If you haven't taken detailed notes from classroom lectures and reading assignments all semester, then you have
more of a problem. It is extremely difficult at the last minute
to catch up on all that material. If you've gotten yourself
into this situation, then you should probably take the gamble and read only certain chapters or assignments carefully.
If there's time, try to skim as many readings as possible.

To skim a text, read some or all of the following parts
of the text:

- Introductions and conclusions
- Summary paragraphs that summarize large portions
  of the text (Usually you can find these at the end of
  a large chunk of text, before a new subject heading.
  They will often be preceded with phrases like, "To
  sum up" or "Thus far we have seen.")
- Chapter titles and subtitles
- Any words or phrases that are in bold, in italics, or
  underlined
- Captions for diagrams and photographs

- The first or last line of all paragraphs
- NOTE: If a particular word, phrase, or line catches your attention and sounds important, read that entire paragraph or section of text.

Even if you are in this bad a situation and need to cram, you should still make certain you get some sleep. At least if you are well-rested, you can call upon whatever background knowledge you have about the subject to help you in the exam.

On Exam Day

The most crucial thing to remember on the day of the exam is that you set your alarm and give yourself enough time to get ready, especially if your exam is in the morning. More than one student has slept through a major exam, and it's hard to get sympathy from the professor when it happens. If your alarm is unreliable, or if you have the habit of turning it off in your sleep or hitting the snooze button, then set several alarms. You may want to have a friend or relative give you a wake up call.

When you take a shower that morning, try talking about some of the key terms or general themes you've prepared on the Master-List. This serves as a mental exercise to get your brain warmed up and focused on the subject matter.

If your exam is in the afternoon or evening, you can take some time in the morning to read over your Master-Lists. But don't overburden yourself. A final read-through should be all you need to put you in the right frame of mind for the exam. Don't spend this time trying to memorize or learn new material. After the read-through, do something to take your mind off the exam, such as taking a walk or watching television.

Make certain you know exactly when and where an exam will be given.

On the day of the test, eat a high carbohydrate meal; carbohydrates, as many athletes know, give your body an energy boost. (A great meal to have before an exam is macaroni and cheese, because you get a mix of carbohydrates and protein.) Don't eat too large a meal, though, because it may make you sleepy.

Be sure you know exactly where the exam is being given and leave yourself enough time to get there. Try to get to an exam about fifteen minutes before it is scheduled to start. That will ensure you don't arrive late, flustered and out of breath because you've had to hurry to be there. You also want to guarantee you have the benefit of the entire allotted time, from the first minute to the last.

Bring several pens of blue or black ink, or pencils and a sharpener if it is a standardized test, and a good watch. You might also want, if you are allowed, to bring some gum, candy, or a drink. Verify that your watch is in working order or that there is a clock in the room, as it is crucial for you to keep track of time during the exam. If you need special tools, such as charts, a compass, or a calculator, make certain you have them ready and they are working properly.

When you get to the exam, choose your seat carefully. You might, for example, want to sit near a window so that you can look up every so often and take a break. You might want to sit where you can see the clock so that you can keep time.

Set an alarm and/or take extra efforts to make certain you get up in time for the exam, such as having a friend call or stop by.

Before the exam begins, avoid talking about anything related to the test with other students, especially alarmists and panickers. You can sit at your desk and glance over your Master-Lists or a last-minute cram sheet if you've made one. But don't get involved in a detailed question and answer session with other students; it's really too late to study or learn any major point. Moreover, if you listen to someone else, you risk becoming confused about a point about which you were previously quite confident. This will only serve to make you feel more anxious about the exam. Stay relaxed and calm so you can take the exam with a clear head.

Sample Study Schedule to Prepare for Four Major Exams

	Mon.	Tues.	Wed.	Thurs.	Fri.	Sat.	Sun.
9-10:00	*Meet with professors to talk about exams*	English Class	*Gym/ Exercise*	English Class	*Gym/ Exercise*	*Work with History Master lists*	*Work with Psychology Master lists*
10-11:00	Psych 101 Class	↓	Psych 101 Class	↓	Psych 101 Class		
11-12:00	*Meet with professors to talk about exams*	*Go to library to read more on English*	*Go to library to read more on History*	*Go to library to read more on Biology*	*Go to library and read more about Psych*		
12-1:00						↓	↓
1-2:00	**L**	**U**	**N**	**C**	**H** ──────────────→		
2-3:00	*Get notes together*	Biology Class	*Meet w/ study partners*	Biology Class	*Meet w/ study partners*	*Work with Biology Master lists*	*Meet with study groups or go to gym*
3-4:00	History Class	↓	History Class	↓	History Class		
4-5:00	*Read over all English notes*	*Read over all History notes*	*Read over all Biology notes*	*Read over all Psychology notes*	*Work with English Master lists*		
5-6:00						↓	
6-7:00	**D**	**I**	**N**	**N**	**E**	**R** ──────────────→	
7-8:00						*Go to a movie; relax*	*Run through cue cards*
8-9:00	*Create Master lists*	*Create Master lists*	*Create Master lists*	*Create Master lists*	*More work with English Master lists*		
9-10:00							
10-11:00							
11-12:00		*If done with work, use this time to relax.*					

Study Schedule and Checklist
Before You Begin Studying (Before Classes End)

- Get information from the professor on exam content and format.
- Try to get sample tests.
- Find out date, time, and location of the exam.
- If you want to, try to find a study group with other hard-working and intelligent students.

Five to Seven Days Prior to Exam

- Sit down and read through all notes from classroom lectures and reading assignments.
- Create the three Master-Lists (key terms, general themes and topics, related concepts). Take about four to six hours per subject to do this.

Two to Five Days Prior to Exam

- Work extensively and repeatedly with the Master-Lists:
  — Quiz yourself on each Master-List for each subject every day.
  — Work with cue cards and use other memorization techniques to learn key terms.
  — Take notes on general themes and talk your way through possible essays.
  — Study list of related concepts.
- See your professor to ask last-minute questions if you have them.
- Meet with study group or partners if you opt to do this.

- Read other sources if time allows.
- Make certain you know where to go for the exam. Confirm the day, time, and location. If you are unfamiliar with the test site, go there sometime before the test day so you can see exactly where it is and how much time it takes to get there.

The Night Before the Exam

- Do one final read-through of the Master-Lists.
- Talk your way through possible essays.
- Make a cram sheet of terms you still can't get down.
- Relax: See a movie or watch TV.
- Get together materials to bring to the exam: pens (that work), your watch (that works), candy, gum, a drink, your final cram sheet, other materials you may need (such as a calculator, books, etc.).
- Get a good night's sleep.
- SET YOUR ALARM BEFORE GOING TO SLEEP!

The Day of the Exam

- Talk about some key terms and general themes in the shower as an exam day warm-up.
- Eat a meal heavy in carbohydrates.
- If you have an afternoon or evening exam, you can take time in the morning to do a final read-through of your Master-Lists.
- Make certain you bring writing utensils and a watch to the exam.
- Get to the exam early to choose a good seat.

The Week of Exams

	Mon.	Tues.	Wed.	Thurs.	Fri.	Sat.	Sun.
9-10:00	Work with English and History Master lists (Quiz self)	Work again with Biology and Psychology Master lists	English Exam	Biology Exam			
10-11:00							
11-12:00							
12-1:00							
1-2:00	**L**	**U**	**N**	**C**	**H**		
2-3:00	Work with Biology and Psychology Master lists (Quiz self)	Last run-through of English Master lists	History Exam	Psych 101 Exam			
3-4:00							
4-5:00							
5-6:00							
6-7:00	**D**	**I**	**N**	**N**	**E**	**R**	
7-8:00	Meet with study group or go to library	Last run-through of History Master lists	Last run-throughs of Biology and Psychology Master lists	Celebrate! Treat yourself to a reward			
8-9:00							
9-10:00							
10-11:00							
11-12:00	*Relax: watch TV or listen to music*						

Keep yourself in prime physical condition; eat well and get regular sleep. The night before an exam, try to relax.

Where to Work: Finding a Comfortable Study Space

Many people seem to think that the only way to study is at a bare desk, with a hard-backed chair, in some minuscule study cubicle in the library. While this setting does wipe out any outside distraction, it's such a gloomy, sterile atmosphere that it turns studying into a form of medieval torture. Studying just doesn't have to be that depressing.

Since you will spend long hours reading over your notes, creating and working with the Master-Lists, you may as well make yourself comfortable. If you work in a space where you are relaxed and feel at home, you will study more often and more effectively. Study anywhere you feel comfortable — in your room, in bed, at the library, in an empty classroom, at a café, outside, in the park — provided that you do two things: 1) minimize outside distractions, and 2) promise yourself to make a change if you don't get the work done.

In choosing a place, consider the amount of outside distractions — such as friends stopping by, the phone ringing, loud music — and do what you can to minimize them. Even the library may not be distraction-free; if everyone

Choose a place to study in which you feel comfortable and can avoid distractions. If you are not working productively, make a change.

you know goes there to study, you may spend more time chatting with friends than working. You can, though, minimize the distraction by avoiding the main study lounge and finding a quieter section of the library, where you won't run into many people you know.

There's nothing wrong with studying in your room so long as you get work done. Your room is, after all, the space where you are most at home. However, you will need to minimize distractions. If you are frequently interrupted by the phone, turn the ringer off; if friends frequently disturb you, keep the door closed.

If you decide to study in your room, it's a good idea to designate a spot as your main work space. Your desk is probably the best place. However, your room need not have a sterile, austere atmosphere. Since it's your room, you can personalize it by hanging up posters or photographs.

You can even listen to music while you study, just as long as it doesn't distract you. Listening to something that you are very familiar with will distract you less than something brand new. If you study outside your room, you can try bringing a portable tape or CD player with headphones along and listening to relaxing music. That's one way to make wherever you study feel a little more like home.

Whatever study space you choose, try to do most of your work there. This will help make studying more of a habit. Arriving at that space — whether it's your desk in your room or your favorite spot in the library — alerts you to the fact that it is time to work. You can begin work more easily in a familiar setting than you can in a strange environment.

You can also designate different places for different subjects. For example, you might decide to prepare for your English exam in one location, and for a science exam somewhere else. You can also find different locations for each step in the test preparation process outlined earlier. You might, for example, read over and reorganize your notes in one spot, and quiz yourself on them somewhere else. Finding a variety of locations does make the process less tedious.

Sometimes, for whatever reason, you'll find it difficult to pay attention. When this happens, a simple change of scene may be all you need to refocus on your work. If you've been studying at your desk, go out somewhere, to a coffee shop or the library, and see if you get more done. However, if you find you consistently don't get a great deal of work done, make a more permanent change. If, for example, you are so relaxed studying in your room that you always fall asleep, then that's probably not the best place for you to work.

Remember, pick a work space where you feel relaxed and comfortable, but one where you also get work done. This means being honest with yourself. Only you know whether you are studying effectively; if you aren't, then you need to initiate changes.

Battling the Enemies:

Fighting Fatigue, Stress, and Procrastination

*I*t's one thing to set a strict regimen for yourself as you approach an exam; sticking to it, though, is another matter. There are a variety of factors that can keep you from working productively; they can even stop you from working at all. You must fight and overcome these psychological obstacles in order to put all of your effort into making the most of test training.

Fighting Fatigue

It might sound like a joke, but many students feel so tired they can't think clearly and some can't help falling asleep while studying for exams; this is a serious problem that can plague your efforts to train for an exam. The need to sleep is powerful — and to fight it, you need to take equally strong measures. Here are a few important suggestions.

Get enough sleep at night.   There's a simple reason why so many students fall asleep while studying, and it's not necessarily boredom. They're just tired. Of course, it's difficult when you are a student to get a good night's sleep all the time, and you shouldn't expect to. However, don't make a habit of staying up late all the time. Try as often as possible to get six to eight hours of sleep a night, especially when preparing for an exam. You might think you should sleep less before an exam so that you can have extra time to study. That's a big mistake, though, because as it gets later and you get more tired, you study much less effectively, not really retaining what you are reading. Stay on a regular sleep schedule throughout the semester, including when you are preparing for exams. You'll need all your energy for the exam itself.

Don't get too much sleep.   You might not realize it, but there is such a thing as *too much sleep*. For most people, six to eight hours of sleep a night is sufficient. If you get more sleep than your body needs, you can feel sleepy all day long.

Exercise regularly.   If you exercise regularly, you'll sleep better at night and be more energized during the day. That means you'll be more focused on your classes and your studies.

Become alarmed.   If you tend to fall asleep while studying, set an alarm. You can purchase an inexpensive travel clock or wristwatch equipped with an alarm and have it nearby while you study. The alarm should be loud enough to wake you up but quiet enough not to disturb those around you. If possible, set the alarm to go off every fifteen minutes. If you can't set it to go off regularly, set it for a specific time (such as a half-hour after you've begun studying) and continue to reset it each time it goes off. And as we said earlier, absolutely make certain you have a trustworthy alarm for the day of an exam.

Arrange wake-up calls or visits. If you don't trust an alarm, have a friend check on you every so often. The easiest method is to arrange to study together; that way you can keep an eye on each other and keep each other awake. Of course, you have to be careful that you both don't fall asleep at the same time, and also that you don't spend too much time chatting. If you are studying in your room, you can have a friend or relative give you a phone call every hour or so to check up on you. Having an alarm and a back-up call on the day of an exam will ensure you won't sleep through that important event.

Take breathers. If you become too comfortable while studying, it's easy to fall asleep. You should plan to get up and walk around at regular intervals — preferably outside. While fresh air can do wonders for waking you up, limit your walks to just a few minutes. When you return to studying, you'll feel revived and better able to focus.

> Make efforts to ensure you stay awake and alert while studying. Get enough sleep regularly — but not too much sleep. Set alarms, plan visits from friends, or take breathers to make certain you don't nod off while working.

Stay actively involved. The more engaged in the material you are, the less likely you'll succumb to sleep. Rather than just reading the words on the page, follow the test preparation strategies outlined here that encourage you to do something active.

Don't get too comfortable. It's important to be comfortable while you study because the more relaxed you are, the more open your mind will be. Additionally, being comfortable makes studying less tedious. However, there is such a thing as being too comfortable. If you find yourself constantly falling asleep, you should change your study habits. For example, if you study on a couch or bed, you might need to sit at a desk, where it is more difficult to fall asleep. If you listen to music, you might need to change your selection to something that will keep you up rather than lull you to sleep. Remember, study in an atmosphere you feel relaxed in, but not so much so that you cannot stay awake.

Putting Off Panic

There's no question that preparing for and taking examinations is stressful. However, when stress becomes panic, it is a serious problem, one that plagues many students. Before an exam, panic can keep you from studying effectively; in the midst of an exam, it can mean the difference between success and failure. Following are some strategies for fighting panic, before and during an examination.

Have a Plan of Attack

One important antidote to panic is having a clear, well-thought-out plan of attack. Not having a plan is like going on a trip without a map — you worry about where you're going and, before you know it, you're lost. When preparing for and taking exams, you also need a solid plan of attack; without one, your studying feels aimless, and you continually wonder if what you are doing is effective. However, when you have a reliable strategy, you feel more in control of the situation and more confident about your abilities. You're probably thinking, "Great, where do I get a plan of attack?" You've got it already — the strategies you've been reading about in this book. So remind yourself every once in a while that you have a plan of attack that will keep you on the path to exam success.

Remember the Big Picture

One major cause of panic is the tendency to blow the significance of exams completely out of proportion, to think of each exam as a matter of ultimate success or failure, life or death. It's extremely important, therefore, that you put the experience into perspective by remembering the big picture. A single examination is only a small part of your overall educational experience and an even more minuscule part of your life. In future years, no one is ever going to ask you how you did on a specific exam in school. You probably won't even remember the exam yourself. Moreover, doing poorly on an examination is not a reflection on you as a person. It's not even a question of intelligence. Some people are simply better at taking exams than others because they've developed successful test-taking skills — skills that you can also learn. If you screw up on one exam, that's no sign you'll screw up on future ones. And if you do find you continue to do poorly, you can seek help. Most colleges, for example, offer special tutoring services. You can work regularly with a tutor and, most likely, improve your examination performance.

Avoid Alarmists

At all costs, stay away from the alarmists. These are other students who, completely stressed out themselves, try to pass their panic on to you. What is truly alarming is how successful they can be at shaking your own confidence. Once they approach you and convey their own fears and worries, you'll find you too start to get nervous. Panic is infectious; before you know it, you'll be freaking out right alongside them.

Be especially wary of rumors you might hear about the level of difficulty of an upcoming examination or about specific questions that will possibly be included. Chances are these are just rumors. If you let them sidetrack you from your own study preparations, you'll be needlessly wasting time.

Avoid alarmists as much as possible, especially in the days before an exam. If an alarmist corners you and asks how you feel about the exam, you can politely say you are studying as best you can and don't want to think about what is on the exam until you get there.

You particularly want to avoid talking to alarmists right before an examination begins. Many will get to the examination room early and ask fellow students to explain things they don't understand but fear will be on the test. There's really no point that late in the game trying to guess what will be on the exam and have someone explain various terms to you; this only gets everyone into a nervous frenzy just as the examination is being passed out. If you get to the examination room several minutes before the test begins, don't talk about the test or the material with other people. The last thing you need to worry about before an exam begins is how much someone else understands. Stay calm and focus your thoughts on what you've already studied.

> Having a set plan of action and keeping things in perspective can help minimize stress and panic. Taking breaks and practicing meditation and relaxation exercises can also help calm you. Whatever you do, avoid alarmists — those students prone to panic themselves.

Take Breathers

Studying for and taking examinations is a physically and mentally exhausting process. It's crucial that you give yourself frequent breaks to help you release tension and relax. Don't study for more than two hours without taking a breather. Take a short walk, stretch your muscles, and give yourself a temporary break from studying. Even a ten- or fifteen-minute break can help you feel revived.

It's just as important that you take a breather while taking an examination. If you are not worried about the time, you can take a short break in the middle of the exam by asking to be excused to get a drink or go to the bathroom. If you don't want to leave the room, you can take a breather right at your seat. Put your pen down and give your hands a short rest. Take your eyes off the exam booklet and look out the window or around the room; just make certain you don't look anywhere near another person's paper, or you might be accused of cheating. Lift your arms in the air to stretch your back muscles and roll your head around to ease tension in your neck. Take several really deep breaths. A breather like this only needs to take about thirty seconds, but it will help you remain calm and focused during the exam.

RELAXATION EXERCISE

Sit in a chair with a firm back and place your hands, palms up, on your thighs. Close your eyes, and take deep breaths. Concentrate for a few moments only on your breathing, on the feeling of the air going in and out of your lungs. Next, picture yourself someplace you've been where you felt safe and happy. See yourself there. Use all your senses. Remember the sights, smells, and sounds of being there. Think about this scene for several moments, continuing to breathe deeply. Enjoy the feeling of safety and serenity you know while you are there. At the same time, know that you can always return here, where you feel safe and happy, when you need to. Sit for as long as you like in this place. When you are ready to leave, count to ten and then open your eyes.

As you practice this exercise, you'll be able to experience that feeling of safety and happiness more and more quickly — in as little as thirty seconds — just by closing your eyes and breathing deeply. Even during an exam, you can take thirty seconds to close your eyes, breathe deeply, and relax.

Practice Relaxation Exercises

There are many relaxation techniques that psychologists and therapists teach people to help them cope with stress and panic. You can use these same techniques while studying for and even during an exam. If you are particularly prone to stress, you may want to buy a book or tape that teaches meditation and relaxation exercises and practice them all semester.

Maintaining Motivation

Just because you set out a rigid schedule to train for exams, by no means are you going to actually want to follow it and do all of the work necessary to prepare. Why would you? It is, after all, hard work. Not only that, it is hard work with extra pressure, which makes the whole experience all the more unappealing. Those negative feelings about the study process can lead you to procrastinate. Procrastination basically means finding ways to put off doing something you don't want to do. You might find yourself coming up with a variety of creative rationalizations for putting off the work. You might, for example, convince yourself you still have plenty of time, and that it makes more sense to wait another day to begin studying so it will all be fresh in your mind. Before you know it, it's the night before exams, and you're in a panic.

To fight the temptation to procrastinate, you first need to catch yourself doing it. Once you set that study schedule, make it your goal to follow it. Don't stray from it for any reason, especially for a "rationalization" you suddenly come up with on your own.

Avoid fellow procrastinators. These are other students who try to do the rationalizing for you. They might offer all kinds of tempting activities to do instead of studying. Again, once you make your study schedule, follow it, and don't listen to advice or suggestions from anyone else.

Continually reminding yourself of the importance of studying and keeping up with your schedule may help you get to work — but that mental coaching might not be enough. You can, though, promise yourself extra rewards that will serve as additional motivation. For each day on your study schedule, you can plan to do something fun or relaxing when you've completed the work for that day. For example, if you schedule in several hours to read and reorganize notes for a course, when you are finished with that task, you can then do something you enjoy. You can read a book, watch TV, go out to eat with friends, or just relax. When you sit down to do the work for the day, remind yourself of the fun activities waiting for you when you are finished.

However, even with the promise of free time as a reward, you may still find it difficult to get motivated and begin working. You can provide yourself with additional rewards as you study. Set small goals, and reward yourself each time you fulfill them. For example, if you have several hours blocked off for preparing Master-Lists, promise yourself a snack after you've worked for two hours. This will at least get you started.

These rewards don't need to be extravagant. A reward can simply be a short break to do something you like — getting ice cream, talking on the phone, going for a walk, listening to music, whatever. Just make certain the

Keep yourself motivated and battle procrastination. Set a rigid study regimen and stick to it. Don't rationalize — or let others rationalize for you — putting off your studying and preparing for exams. Promise yourself breaks and rewards to keep motivated — and an extra special reward when the exam is over.

"reward" time is a short break lasting no more than fifteen to thirty minutes.

This reward system is particularly helpful if you have to spend long hours at work. If you think of yourself as slaving away for many long hours, it will be extremely difficult to motivate yourself to begin work. However, if you divide your studying into several small blocks of time and promise yourself a small reward at the completion of each one, it will be much easier to get started. You know then that when you sit down to work, a reward of some kind is not all that far away.

You can also promise yourself an extra special reward at the end of an exam — like a new CD or a fun evening out. These rewards will help you get through the especially difficult training period leading up to the exam.

The Test Run:

Strategies for Taking Exams

p until now, we've talked extensively about preparing for an exam. If you follow the strategies described in this book, you'll be able to enter an exam ready to answer almost any question you might encounter. You've not only re-examined the material from the course, you've thought about it and worked with it actively. As a result, you've absorbed and retained information, and you can apply that information to specific questions that you've already anticipated. Having done this extensive preparation, you should now feel confident about your mastery of the subject. That confidence will help you perform efficiently and productively — without stress or panic — on the actual test.

The bulk of this book has looked at exam preparation strategies because they are the true key to test-taking success. However, there are certain additional tips you can follow while taking the test that can help improve your performance. This last chapter discusses those techniques.

Before You Begin: Look at the Big Picture

When you get the exam, don't just dive in and begin answering questions. Instead, take a moment to glance through the entire exam to see how it is structured and get a sense of the kinds of questions waiting for you. That way you can devise a plan of attack that ensures you use the time efficiently. Remember, having a plan of attack minimizes the tendency to panic midway through the exam.

Look through the exam to see how many sections there are, the type of questions that are included, and the point values for each section. Then, create a rough schedule for yourself, allotting a certain amount of time for each section depending on how many points it is worth and the level of difficulty.

Obviously, the more points a section is worth, the more time you should devote to it. For example, if an hour-long exam is divided into a short answer section worth fifty points and an essay portion worth fifty points, then you should spend an equal amount of time for each section, thirty minutes. However, if the short answer section is worth only thirty points and the essay portion is worth seventy, then you should spend much more time on the essay section. You'd probably divide your time with about forty minutes for the essay and twenty for the short answer section.

But you should also take into account the levels of difficulty of each section when planning how much time to

Start any exam by getting a sense of the big picture. Look through the entire exam to see what you are in for. Try to assess how much time you need to devote to different sections, and devise a plan of attack that ensures you use the time efficiently.

spend. For example, you may find short answer questions much easier than writing essays. If that is the case, you can allot additional time to the essay portion of the exam.

The other advantage to looking at the entire exam beforehand is that you won't have any surprises waiting for you. It is extremely helpful, for example, to know if there is an essay section following the multiple choice questions. That way, while you are answering the multiple choice questions, you can also be thinking about how you will approach the essay when you get to it. You might also come across short answer questions that include terms or give you ideas for things to include in the essay.

Strategies for Answering Short Answer Questions

As we saw earlier in the book, there are several types of short answer questions that are commonly asked on examinations. Although there are some specific considerations for each type of question, in general you can follow the same overall technique.

Read the Directions

Students often make the mistake of diving right into the questions without reading the directions. The directions often include important information you need to know *before* you start answering questions — that's why they're included on the examination in the first place. For example, you may not be expected to answer all questions on the exam but have a choice. You won't know that, though, unless you read the instructions. It would really be unfortunate for you to take the time to answer all fifty questions, when the directions told you to choose only thirty. The directions might also indicate whether you are penalized for incorrect answers. If you are penalized, then you won't want to guess as often. In general, get all the facts about the examination before jumping in to answer questions.

Read Each Question Very Carefully

With all short answer questions, it is extremely important that you read each one very carefully. Make certain you read the entire question and, if it is a multiple choice question, all the possible choices as well. Don't read the first few words or skim the question and think you know the answer. Sometimes the wording of a question (or the choices on a multiple choice question) will look familiar and therefore you'll assume you know the answer; however, when you take the time to read the question, you may find that even if an answer sounds right, it's still not correct.

When students get short answer questions wrong, it's often the fault of "trick words" that they've overlooked. These

Take exams strategically; keep a clear head, watch the time, and pace yourself. Don't panic.

are crucial words tucked into the question that completely determine the correct answer but are easily overlooked.

For example, look at the following question:

Which of the following is not by William Shakespeare?
a. Romeo and Juliet
b. Troilus and Cressida
c. Doctor Faustus
d. A Midsummer Night's Dream
e. Love's Labours Lost

If you read that question too quickly, you can easily skip over the word "not" and instead think it is asking you to identify a play that Shakespeare did write. And if you don't take the time to read all of the choices, you might first see *Romeo and Juliet*, know it is by Shakespeare, and assume that is the correct answer. However, if you read the question carefully, then you see the question is asking which play is NOT written by Shakespeare; that small, three-letter word makes all the difference. And if you read all of the choices, you then see that there are three other plays in addition to *Romeo and Juliet* that Shakespeare did write. (By the way, the correct answer is "c.")

Always be on the lookout for these "trick words"; if you see one, underline it in the question so you can keep it in

> Trick words frequently tucked into exam questions:
>
> | | |
> |---|---|
> | *all* | *never* |
> | *always* | *none* |
> | *except* | *not* |
> | *less* | *some* |
> | *more* | *sometimes* |

mind as you attempt to determine the answer. And never assume that just because a true/false statement or a possible choice in a multiple choice question looks familiar that it is necessarily true or correct. There could be one word tucked into the sentence that invalidates the entire statement.

Watch the Time and Pace Yourself

Time is of the essence, especially on an exam. You don't have all day to mull over every question. You've therefore got to watch the clock and pace yourself throughout the exam to make certain you get to all of the questions.

When you first get the exam, look at the total number of questions and how much time you have to answer them. You can then figure out approximately how much time you have to answer each one; of course, you may spend more time on the harder questions and less time on the easy ones, but it should average out. Check the time frequently as you proceed. It's a good idea to get in the habit of checking your watch every time you turn the page of

> Read all directions and questions carefully. Make certain you understand them completely. Try to translate difficult questions into everyday, conversational speech. Watch out for "trick" words that might be easily overlooked.

the exam. Monitor your progress and look at how many more questions you have to go. If you find you are going too slowly, then try to pick up the pace.

Difficult questions will require more thought and therefore more time. When you get stuck on a particular question, you risk using up time that could be spent answering easier questions — the ones where you immediately know the answer without a doubt. If you come across a very difficult question, skip it; that way you make certain you have the time to get to all of the questions you can answer easily and therefore get all those points. Put a circle around the difficult questions so you can find them when you want to go back. After having completed all of the questions you can answer without a problem, if time allows, you can go back to the tricky questions and take more time to think about them.

Intelligent Guessing

Chances are you are not going to know the answer to every question on an examination. However, no one says you have to. On a short answer question, you can always take a guess. And if you guess intelligently, you have a decent shot at getting it right.

Fill-in-the-Blank Questions.   It's most difficult to make guesses on fill-in-the-blank questions because you need to furnish the answer; you aren't given a selection of choices as you would on a multiple choice question. That means you either know the answer or you don't. However, you can perhaps narrow down the possible answers for yourself. Try to identify a general theme that the question reflects. Then think about the key terms you identified on your Master-List, as relating to that same theme. There's a strong chance that one of those terms will be the correct answer to fill in the blank. You can also look for and underline the key terms within the statement. Then think about your Master-List of Related Concepts. Are the key terms in the statement part of a group of related concepts? What were the other key terms you listed in the same group? One of them is likely to be the right answer.

True/False Questions.   It almost always pays to guess on a true/false question because you have a fifty-fifty chance of getting it right. If you are uncertain about how to respond, try to test out the statement by finding specific cases that support or counter the statement. For example, if the statement asserts that a particular phenomenon is *always* true, you only need to think of a single case when that statement is *not true* and the answer will have to be false. Similarly, if the word "never" or "sometimes" is included, you only need to think of a single case when the statement is true, and it will also have to be false.

128

When you come up with specific cases that support your guess, you can be confident your answer is correct.

Multiple Choice Questions. The key to guessing on multiple choice questions is to eliminate as many of the possible choices as you can. With each one you eliminate, you raise the odds that you will pick a correct response. If you can narrow it down to two choices, then you've got a fifty-fifty chance of getting it right — the same odds as on a true/false question.

There will usually be at least one choice you can eliminate right off the bat because it is obviously wrong. After that, you can examine each choice and see if there is anything incorrect within the answer itself. If the choice can't stand on its own as an accurate statement, then it is probably not a correct answer to the question and you can eliminate it. For example, a possible choice might include a key term with the wrong definition of that term. In that case, you know it won't be the right response. Finally, you can eliminate choices that don't reflect the same general theme as the question. A choice that relates to a completely different theme most likely will not be the correct answer. Watch out for choices that, on their own, are correct and accurate statements; they aren't always the correct answer to the question.

Once you narrow down the responses to two options, don't spend too much time pondering and evaluating which one is the right choice. Just go with your gut instinct; these first impressions are usually right. And once you've put in your guess, don't go back and change it unless you later figure out the correct response with

Just because a choice is itself an accurate statement doesn't mean it is correct in the context of the question.

absolute certainty. Sometimes, for example, a later question will include information that sparks your memory or helps you figure out the answer to an earlier question. If that happens, go back and change the answer. Otherwise, forget about the question and forge ahead.

Many multiple choice questions include the options "all of the above" and "none of the above." When these statements are included, it becomes much easier to make a guess. Look at the other choices. If you identify a single one that you think is an accurate answer to the question, then you can confidently eliminate the "none of the above" option. By the same token, if you are only allowed to include one answer, and you find all the choices are accurate answers to the question, then the "all of the above" option must be the correct answer.

Matching Questions.   In a way, matching sections are just a series of multiple choice questions. Each term or phrase from the first column has a series of possible answers in the second column. On most matching exercises each term has only one counterpart; you cannot use terms in the second column twice. That means for each one you correctly match, you cut down the possible remaining choices. When you have a matching section, first match all of the items that you can do easily and that you are absolutely certain

Guess intelligently. Use what you do know to figure out what you don't.

are correct. You can then focus on the remaining terms ar choices. Your chances of guessing correctly improve wit each correct match you make. Start out putting togeth the terms that you strongly think might go togethe remember, for each correct match, you limit the choices for the remaining items and improve the chances you w guess correctly. As with guessing on multiple choice que tions, try to remember your lists of topics and related cor cepts to identify terms and ideas that go together.

Use Visualization

You might find, in the midst of an exam, that you've forgo ten some piece of information you are certain you studie This can be particularly frustrating because you know yo know the answer, but you just can't remember it. That mear it's stuck somewhere in your long-term memory and you a having trouble accessing it. Close your eyes and picture tl page from your notes or the Master-List on which the info mation is included. Try to "see" the page in your mind. Ca you "read" in your mind the information on the pag Picture yourself studying those notes wherever you actual studied. Sometimes putting yourself into the context in whi you originally read or were exposed to some piece of info mation will help you remember it. If none of that works, sk the question and move on to others. You may find that as yo

answer other questions, you manage to remember the information you needed for an earlier one. The memory is a mysterious mechanism; sometimes it resists pressure on it until you are distracted.

A Word on Penalties

On some examinations, you are penalized more for putting in an incorrect answer than for leaving the question blank. On those tests, you might not want to guess as often. However, if you can narrow down your choices to two or even three possibilities, then it is usually to your advantage to try to guess, since the odds are in your favor. Additionally, if you get one "guess" right, you'll usually get enough points that will outweigh several incorrect guesses, whereas leaving a question blank won't earn you any points at all.

If You Have Trouble Understanding the Question

Read over the question a few times and see if you can at least get the gist of it. Don't worry about the specific words in the question that you don't know. Focus instead on what the question is essentially asking of you. Is it that you furnish a key term? Provide a definition of a term? Provide an example or illustration of some idea? Figure out the exception to some rule? If you can figure out the nature of the question, you may be able to narrow down the possible answers.

When you read over the question, underline any key terms you can identify. What general theme or topic is associated with those key terms? If you think more about that general theme, what related concepts or issues come to

mind? Do any of these topics seem to tie in to the question? If it is a multiple choice question, look at the various answers. Do you understand the choices? Do any of them contain key terms with which you are familiar? Sometimes, even if you don't understand a specific question, you may be able to make a guess based on your overall knowledge of the general theme to which the question relates.

Strategies for Answering Essay Questions

Read the Directions Carefully

Before you even begin to read the essay question(s) on an examination, make certain you read any instructions. You need to find out, for example, how many essays you are supposed to write. Are you expected to answer all the questions, or do you have a choice? If there is a choice, how many essays do you need to answer? Are there any other requirements regarding specific things to include in your response? Requirements described in the directions can seriously affect the way in which you approach the essay questions, so it is essential to read them before you begin to write.

Read the Question(s) Carefully

As with multiple choice and short answer questions, it is crucial that you read the essay questions very carefully. Don't begin writing until you have read the questions in their entirety and are certain you understand them. Essay questions will not always be written in a direct, clear, or straightforward manner and you may have to think about what exactly is being asked of you. Sometimes, for example, teachers write lengthy essay questions that include more information than the actual question, such as quotations or anecdotes. Or there may be several questions related to a common topic, all of which you are expected to address in your response. There are also essay questions that are not even phrased as questions, but tell you to "discuss" or "address" some topic. Read carefully and try to identify exactly what you need to address or respond to in your essay. Read the question and underline any lines or phrases that specifically indicate points you are to address.

If You Must Make a Choice

On many exams, rather than having to write in a response to a single essay question, you will be given a choice of questions. Make certain you choose carefully so that you pick the question for which you can write the most impressive essay possible. Don't just begin writing on the first question. For each question, take a few moments to consider your knowledge of the topic, and the specific points or concepts you would address as part of your essay. You might even jot down a few notes next to each question indicating your thoughts about the question. Choose the essay question about which you have the most to say and feel most comfortable and confident about answering. Just don't waste much time agonizing over the decision — time that could be spent actually writing. Look at the questions, think about each one for a few seconds, make your decision and go with it.

Once you've made your decision, try your best to stick with it. Students sometimes lose their nerve halfway through their response and decide to try answering a different question. But they then have only a little bit of time left, making it difficult, if not impossible, to write an adequate response. You are generally better off sticking with your first choice and doing the best you can; even if you've gotten stuck midway, you've probably written more than you'd be able to if you started on another essay question. However, if you still have a great deal of time left and find you truly cannot continue writing about a certain topic, then you can take the risk and switch questions.

Connect the Essay Question to a General Theme or Concept

As we discussed earlier, most essay questions relate to fairly broad topics; they therefore reflect general themes from the course, or subjects you listed on your Master-List of Related Concepts. When you consider how to respond to an essay question, first see if it connects with any of the general themes or concepts for the course. If it does, you then can include the various points and/or terms you studied in connection to each theme as part of your preparation for the exam.

If you are lucky, an essay question will mirror a general theme you studied almost exactly. However, the question may not so clearly relate to a specific general theme. It might, for example, draw on several themes from the course. If this is the case, you can still bring in the information you studied in relation to these themes. You probably won't have the time to address all of the specific concepts and terms you connected to those themes, so you'll have to make some educated decisions about what to write about and what to leave out.

The question might be phrased in such a manner that it is not entirely apparent whether or not it relates to a general theme. In this case, look for any key terms from the course that appear in the question. Do those key terms relate to a particular general theme? If they do, then the entire question probably relates somehow to that same theme.

If the Question Is Confusing or Difficult

It's always possible that you'll get a complex question that doesn't tie neatly into a particular theme. The professor may be trying to challenge you, to test your ability to grapple, on the spot, with a very difficult topic. Take a few moments to examine the question and again think carefully about what is being asked of you. Remember, no matter how confusing the question looks, it must somehow tie in with the subject matter of the course. Remind yourself that you've spent a great deal of time immersed in this subject matter, so you are equipped to discuss it. Look at the question for any key terms or phrases you understand and think about the general theme to which they relate. You can sometimes discuss the general theme in a very broad sense and still get partial credit.

Whatever you do, make certain you always write *something*. If you just panic and don't write anything, you are certain to fail. But if you go ahead and write an answer, you can at least get partial credit. Everyone in the class is in the same boat. They're all stuck with the same question and are probably struggling with it as well. Try to write a confident, well-organized response in which you address something that seems related to the question, or to the course material. You'll show the professor you did learn something, which should earn you some credit.

Jot Down a Few Notes

Once you've decided on the essay, take a minute to jot down a few notes in the margin of the exam booklet on what you plan to address in your response. List the basic points, concepts, key terms, and examples you will raise in your essay. If you've identified a general theme that the question relates to, you then just need to replicate the list of related topics you made at home. If this is not the case, brainstorm for a minute and write down your ideas.

After you've written down the main points you plan to include, consider the order in which you will address them. An essay on an exam is no different from a term paper in that you can be strategic in your organization. You want to make certain you begin and end with your most impressive and intelligent points; that way you give a strong opening impression and conclude with a spectacular finish.

But don't spend a great deal of time planning the essay; the bulk of your time should be spent writing. Take just a minute or two to jot down your notes and plan the organization of the essay.

Neatness Counts

If your professor has to struggle to read your essay, he or she is not going to view it very positively, even if you've written a brilliant response. That's why, whether it's fair or not, neatness counts.

Use a black or blue ink pen, but not one that smudges easily. Only write on one side of a page in the exam booklet as the ink can show through the page and make it difficult to read. Most importantly, write as neatly and legibly as possible. If your script is difficult to read, then print. It may take you a little longer to print your response, but it will be neater and therefore ultimately worth the time it takes.

As you are writing, you may find you need to make changes in what you have already written; you might want to cross out a line or a section, or add additional information to a previous paragraph. Make these changes clear. Cross out a section by drawing a line through the material you wish to delete; don't scribble and blot out what you've written. When you want to add a line or passage, use the top margin of the page, circle the passage to be added, and draw an arrow down to the spot in which it should be inserted.

Use a Three-Part Structure

Many students just launch into an essay and write whatever is on their minds without any kind of structure or organization. This makes for a sloppy, unimpressive essay that probably won't impress the professor. Even if a student raises intelligent points in his or her essay, those ideas become lost if there isn't a solid structure to support them.

On an exam, you don't have much time to worry, though, about planning a detailed, complex structure. You can therefore use a standard, three-part structure, the same you would use for a term paper, which includes an introduction, body, and conclusion. This three-part structure particularly lends itself to examination questions because it provides a set formula. You don't have to think hard about the organization; you merely need to plug the relevant information into those three parts.

The Introduction. The introduction is particularly important on an examination because it provides your professor with the first sign of your knowledge of the material and your confidence in the subject matter. If the introduction is clear and intelligent, the professor will gain a favorable impression that will remain with him the entire time he reads your essay.

You don't, however, need to spend a great deal of time writing the introduction. It doesn't have to be especially innovative, creative, or lengthy — it only needs to be a single, short paragraph in which you establish the general focus of the essay. The simplest way to do that is to use information given in the question. Write a few sentences that essentially rephrase and expand on the question. You should also include a thesis statement that summarizes the main idea or central issue of the question. (You can read *Term Paper Secrets* in the Backpack Study Series to learn how to design a thesis statement.) Starting an essay by rephrasing and addressing the question provides you with material for the introduction and, more importantly, gets you started writing. You don't have to agonize over the best way to begin. The question provides you with enough material to get you started, and once you've begun, you'll find it much easier to continue writing.

The introduction on an examination question can also be used strategically. Very often, there are several ways to interpret and approach a particular essay question. You can use the introduction to set the terms by which you plan to address the question. In your introduction, make it very clear how you are interpreting and defining the question. If you make your intention clear from the beginning, your professor will be tapped into your thinking and see where you are going.

The Body.   After the introduction paragraph, you should launch directly into the body of the essay. As with the essay as a whole, it is important that the body be well-organized and clearly structured. Make certain you divide the body into paragraphs, each centering on a specific point that supports the overall topic of the essay. If you've taken a few moments before the exam to jot down your ideas and plan the order in which you will raise them, then you should be able to write an organized body without too much trouble. Whatever you do, don't turn in one long chunk of material that is difficult to read. Make sure the first line of each new paragraph is clearly indented. It's usually more effective in an exam to include many short paragraphs than a few long ones, as it then appears you are raising many different points. At the same time, though, make certain that each paragraph focuses on a very specific point, concept, or example. If you include extraneous information that's off the point, the essay appears unfocused and sloppy.

The Conclusion. On an exam essay, it's as important to include a conclusion as it is an introduction. Some professors only skim essays, especially if they have a heavy load of exams to grade, but they usually read the introduction and the conclusion, so use them to your advantage. While the introduction provides the first impression, the conclusion is the final taste your professor has of your essay, right before he gives it a grade. You don't need to have an especially provocative or creative conclusion. Use the conclusion to summarize the key points you made within the essay. This will emphasize to the professor that you successfully answered the essay question and are knowledgeable of the subject matter. The conclusion doesn't have to be especially long — just a few sentences. Just be sure that you watch the time and leave yourself a few minutes to write the conclusion. If you lose track of time and the exam ends when you are still working on the body, the essay is essentially unfinished and appears tentative and unfocused. But adding a short conclusion demonstrates that you had a plan of attack in mind and successfully completed it.

141

Become a Communication Master

As you write an essay, remind yourself you are writing for a specific audience with a specific purpose in mind — you are writing this essay for your professor, and you are doing it to communicate how much you have learned about the subject. You want to make it crystal clear that you not only learned something, but have mastered the material of the course. That confident attitude should be reflected in the content and style of the essay.

You want to write, first of all, in as clear a manner as possible. If your wording is muddled or confused, your ideas will also be confused. Make certain you describe each point in extensive detail. Anticipate any questions a reader might have about each sentence you write, and proceed to include the answers to those questions. Define any terms you include in explicit detail.

At the same time, adopt a tone that indicates your knowledge of and comfort with the material. Use sophisticated vocabulary and terminology, but not in a forced or incorrect manner. Include as many relevant key terms from the course as possible, along with explanations and definitions of the terms. This demonstrates to the professor how much you have learned from the course. You may even want to underline the key terms you use, so that they will stand out for the professor even if he skims the essay. Feel free to be a name-dropper and bring in other sources you may have read in the course of your studies. Include as much relevant information as you can that will communicate the breadth of your knowledge and learning.

However, you do need to be careful. Don't, under any circumstances, include anything that is incorrect or that you don't fully understand. If you include any incorrect information, it will make a very poor impression; the professor may penalize you severely, even though you have a great deal of other points that are correct. You are better off leaving out a particular term or point altogether than including incorrect information. And while you want to convey the breadth of your knowledge, you don't want to pad the essay with irrelevant details. You can include some points or terms that are related but not central to the essay, but you don't need to throw in the kitchen sink. Don't bring up topics or terms that have absolutely nothing to do with the essay. If you do, the professor will think you don't really understand the question. Just include the points you know are relevant and will impress the professor with your knowledge.

Watch the Time

Check the clock frequently to be sure you have enough time to get all the way through your essay. It's easy to get caught up in a single point, only to find time is running out and you have to rush through the rest of the response. Pace yourself and move quickly; give yourself a certain amount of time to address each point and stick to the schedule.

If you are running out of time, finish whatever point you are on and jump ahead to the conclusion. Make certain you include a conclusion, even if it is just a few sentences. In the conclusion, you might refer to some of the additional points you would have made if you had more time.

On essays and problem sets, keep in mind your goal is to clearly communicate to the teacher your successful mastery of a particular subject.

This will at least let the professor know that you are aware of additional information related to that particular issue.

If you have so little time that you can't complete the essay or write a conclusion, include a brief outline listing the points you planned to address. Include as many key terms and facts as possible in this outline. By doing this, the professor will at least see that you do know something about the subject and might give you partial credit. Include a brief note to the professor in which you apologize for being unable to complete the essay because of lack of time. You might at least get some points for doing this, and every point counts.

Sample Exam Essay Question and Response

Essay Question #1. While many people consider the Middle Ages to have been marked by the same general social character, there is a distinctive shift in the overall mood between the early and latter parts of the period. Write a well-developed essay in which you analyze the social and political changes in the latter half of the Middle Ages. In your answer, discuss how you would generally characterize the second half of the period.

In examining accounts of life in the Middle Ages, one detects a distinctive shift in tone between the earlier and latter halves of the period. While the earlier half is characterized by a tremendous optimism and hope in the future, the latter is marked by an increasing sense of gloom and despair. This shift in the general mood results in large part from the major social and political changes in the second half of the period.

> **Introduction:**
> — Restates the question in your own terms
> — Makes clear your approach to the topic

The twelfth and thirteenth centuries, considered to be the early part of the Middle Ages, were marked by major political and economic developments that ushered in a time of relative stability. The ongoing struggles between the nobility and the throne were at last resolved during the reign of Henry II, who instituted major changes. Instituting a working bureaucracy, Henry successfully collected taxes and kept records of the incoming funds. The economy of the country was at last stabilized, and as trade increased with other countries, England grew richer. This ushered in a construction boom reflected in the rise in towns and cities, the building of the great cathedrals, and the formation of universities. This explosion of extraordinary achievements contributed to a general mood of hope and optimism in the future.

> **Body:**
> — Includes several major points supporting the topic

The latter half of the period, in the fourteenth and fifteenth centuries, however, was marked by a complete shift in mood. Instead of optimism and hope, it was a time of gloom and despair. There are several factors behind this shift. For one, the truce reached between the barons and the crown instituted by Henry II was once again threatened. Edward II and Richard II were comparatively weak kings, unsuccessful at standing up to the nobles. During their reigns, the country was constantly beset by civil war. Both kings were eventually deposed by nobles.

In addition to civil wars, the One Hundred Years' War (1337-1433) was a long, debilitating war. The war began when Edward III claimed he had a right to the French throne through his mother. Although the war was fought entirely on French soil, the English economy was seriously depleted. While people back home were going hungry, bands of English soldiers were ravaging and pillaging the French villages and cities. The war was therefore controversial and very unpopular among many people who saw it as unnecessary. After a series of disastrous battles, the English withdrew and gave up all their claims in France.

— Each paragraph centers on a single point

— Mentions many key terms, which are defined and explained

Another major event that changed the mood was the Black Plague in 1348. The plague spread with astonishing speed and killed off about one third of the general population—a staggering amount. This was responsible in part for creating economic problems. Most of those killed by the plague were poor people; the nobles largely escaped it. There was therefore a major shortage of labor. All building had to stop and farming seriously declined, creating food shortages. In addition to economic problems, the plague generally fostered a sense of despair. People saw death everywhere around them, and became obsessed with it. This is evident in the art and literature of the period, which features the figure of Death in various forms. The _Danse Macabre_, for example, features death striking down various members of society, regardless of age or class.

    Finally, the church instigated a new policy that brought about a major change in people's attitudes toward it. In the fourteenth century, the papacy condoned the sale of pardons and indulgences. The sale was a way you could essentially buy penance for sins you had committed. This meant, in part, that those with money could buy their way into heaven easily, while the poor could not. It also led to a great deal of church corruption, since those selling pardons could blackmail innocent people into buying their wares. In Chaucer's _Canterbury Tales_, the Pardoner is a typical example of a corrupt church official, reflecting the general view among the public of the church in the period. Additionally, many church offices began to be auctioned off to the highest bidder, or went to family members of existing officers. As a result, the general populace began to feel more and more skeptical of the church as a moral institution.

— Written in a confident, knowledgeable tone

    The fourteenth and fifteenth centuries thus saw
several major negative social and political
developments, including the threat to the throne under
weak kings, the Hundred Years' War, the Black Plague,
and increased church corruption. There were other developments as well, including a series of popular rebellions
waged by the exploited lower classes that were often
put down in violent fashion by the throne. The combination of economic turmoil and the harsh reminders of
sudden death all around them quite naturally led people
to feel despair and gloom. This marks a sudden shift
from the general optimism of the earlier half of the
Middle Ages, when political and economic stability and
prosperity had led to great changes.

Conclusion:
— Restates the main points addressed in the essay clearly and concisely
— Mentions additional, related topic not addressed (due to lack of time)
— Clearly indicates the essay is completed

Tips for Doing Complex Problems

For math and science exams on which you must work on a complicated problem and show your work, you can follow many of the same strategies listed for essays. Make certain you read the question(s) very carefully and fully understand them. Try to visualize what the question is asking you; for example, if you are figuring out the surface area of a sphere, picture the sphere in your mind as you read the question. If you must choose a problem, make the choice carefully, choosing the one about which you are most confident in your abilities. The questions may resemble those you've worked on for class assignments, and you'll then have a sense of which ones you can do easily and correctly and which ones are trouble.

The key to these problems, as with essays, is to identify the larger concept to which the problem is related. Just as an essay question will usually tie in with a particular theme or concept from the class, complex problems usually tie in to some specific mathematical/scientific formula, theory, principle, or law — or a combination of several of them. As part of your preparation for the exam, when you prepare the Master-List of Related Concepts, you can try listing these principles with the kinds of questions or problems that they lead to. On the exam, study the question or problem and identify which formulas, theories, laws, or principles you need to invoke to answer the question or solve the problem. Write them down, or

> Learn something from each test you take that can help you on future exams.

take down a few notes on them. Keep looking at and referring to those notes as you work.

Remember to watch the clock to be sure you have enough time to work — and leave yourself enough time for other questions.

After the Exam

Exams can give you valuable insights into your strengths and weaknesses as a test-taker. Whenever possible, examine tests you've taken after they've been graded. If the exam was given during the school semester, your professor will probably give it back to you. If it was a final, you may need to make an appointment with the professor and ask to see your exam.

When you get the exam back, look through it and study any errors you've made. First, make certain you understand why you got points deducted. It's particularly important that you do this if later examinations in the semester will cover the same material. If you don't take the time to learn from your mistakes, you're not going to get those questions right on the final.

You should also try to identify patterns in your errors. Is there a particular type of mistake you were more likely to make? Did you tend to make factual errors, failing to identify and define key terms correctly? Or were your errors more conceptual, involving the way you approached problems and questions? Did you misread or misunderstand the questions? If you can pick out a pattern, you can focus on that particular problem and work to make changes.

You can also try to talk to your professor about the exam. Ask for advice about what you might do in the future to raise your grade. You should particularly talk to the professor if you have failed the exam. Tell the professor you are concerned about your grade and want to know what you might do in the future to improve. By doing this, you demonstrate to the professor that you are not a lazy or uncaring student and that you take the grade very seriously. At the same time, the professor might offer you valuable advice on how to study that can help you on future tests.

Sometimes teachers do make mistakes when they grade exams. However, if you catch an error, you should think first about whether or not it's worth pointing out to the professor. It's generally not worth quibbling over a few points because you create an unfavorable impression; even if you get the points, the professor may be less inclined to give you a high grade for the course. If there was a serious error made in grading your exam, then by all means point it out. However, you should only do this if you are absolutely certain the professor made a mistake. If you challenge a grade and you are not correct, the professor will not take kindly to it.

If you did poorly or failed, don't get too down about it. Remember that this one exam is just a small part of a much bigger picture. Later in your life, no one will have to know what grade you got on a specific test back in school; you probably won't remember it yourself. Try as much as you can to turn it into a learning experience; even if you fail a test, you can gain some knowledge that will help you in the future.

Index

identifying trouble areas with, 43-44
key term relation to, 37-38
Master-List creation for, 20-22, 94
tutoring, to improve exam
performance, 114
typeface, as indicator of key term,
19, 97

V
visualizations
for answering exam questions,
131-132
for enhancing memory, 69-72, 76-78
for improving vocabulary, 88-89
vocabulary improvement. *see also*
memory improvement; words
discovering new words, 81-85
in general, 79-81
learning new words, 85-89

use it or lose it, 90-92
word breakdown, 89-90

W
words. *see also* vocabulary improvement
in academic style, 79-82
for essay questions, 142
as memory associators, 68, 69-71
prefixes and suffixes, 89-90, 91
as retrieval cues, 60-62
"trick words" on exam questions,
124-125
writing
for exam questions, 138, 142
to improve memory, xiii, 64, 65,
87-88
writings, use as information source,
47-48
writing style, of academia, 79-80, 81